ON ACCURACY OF EUROPEAN AI LAW

ON ACCURACY OF EUROPEAN AI LAW

A Proto Manual for Engineers & Legal Scholars Advancing Adjustments for European Regulators

Raphaël Weuts

INTERSENTIA
LEFEBVRE GROUP

Intersentia
Lefebvre Belgium SA
Avenue Jean Monnet 4
1348 Louvain-la-Neuve
Belgium
Email: contact@larcier-intersentia.com

Distribution for the UK, Ireland and
Rest of the World (excl. France, Belgium and Luxembourg)
Ingram Publisher Services UK
1 Deltic Avenue, Rooksley
Milton Keynes MK13 8LD
United Kingdom
Tel: +44 1752 202 301 | Fax: +44 1752 202 331
Email: ipsuk.customercare@ingramcontent.com

Distribution for France and Rest of the World (excl. Ireland and the UK)
Interforum Editis
Avenue de France 92
75013 Paris
France

Distribution for Belgium and Luxembourg
Larcier-Intersentia
Avenue Jean Monnet 4
1348 Louvain-la-Neuve
Belgium

On Accuracy of European AI Law. A Proto Manual for Engineers & Legal Scholars Advancing Adjustments for European Regulators

ISBN 978-1-83970-621-9
D/2026/06040/0139
NUR 820

British Library Cataloguing in Publication Data. A catalogue record for this book is available from the British Library.

If **C**ongruence is the lack of distance between the actual and the optimal place
in the state-space of possible states of the world,

Alignment is the lack of distance between the proxy chosen and the actual global optimum
in the state-space,

and **I**ntelligence is the force that moves us
through the state-space,
perhaps

$$C = \int A \, dI$$

and alignment steers the vector of intelligence
while we ride the waves of the state-space

ABOUT THIS BOOK

A PROPOSAL & A PROTO MANUAL

This book is a living instrument in a fast-evolving field. No expert can oversee the evolutions of the field exhaustively. It is however built on years of research and experience. Where possible I aim to provide nuance and sources for more information in the endnotes. AI regulation changes at an accelerating pace. The field will evolve and this book will become out of date; it likely already was before it was printed; however, it might make getting up to speed faster, for it might educate the reader on where to search for which notions.

FOR WHOM

This book provides (i) an ontology of the dimensions of accuracy derived from descriptive research of technical literature, (ii) an ontology of categories of AI in the European AI Act, (iii) a study of the definition of AI systems, as well as medical AI, in European law, (iv) a mapping of the ontology on accuracy to the requirements different European laws put forth regarding AI systems and models, specified per category of AI, as well as the type of actor (developer, deployer, health institution ...) and (v) advances proposals for mitigation of the gaps that currently seem present in the combined coverage of European AI law.

It could serve for students of AI engineering and law, to bring an understanding of the interplay between technical standards, law, statistics, computer science and goal specification. It entails a proto manual for developers of AI systems, especially regarding medical AI in a European context. It refers extensively to a broad corpus relevant for legal scholars. Finally, it provides concrete options for European AI legislators.

IN CONCRETO

Artificial intelligence does not necessarily do what we want, rather what we ask. This has to do with accuracy, which is not a singular thing. This book analyses the different aspects of accuracy defined in technical literature and which of those are reflected in legal notions of accuracy in the AI Act, GDPR, MDR and GPAI Code of Practice. All aspects of accuracy refer to two things: the distance between two variables and the choice of those two variables. This book identifies five aspects of accuracy: traditional accuracy, input accuracy, feedback, proxy choice and subgoal robustness. The work illustrates that the notion of accuracy of the AI Act is defined in the AI Act in combination with harmonised standards and the GPAI Code of Practice. The findings illustrate that the AI Act differs in its coverage of the aspects of accuracy in function of both the category of AI system, as well as the actor involved. The work identifies that the GDPR does not cover all aspects. In addition, the GPAI Code of Practice, differs in its coverage depending on whether the GPAI model is considered to have systemic risk. This book provides concrete examples for all aspects of accuracy and performs a deeper case study on the AI Act. It illustrates potential gaps, the most pertinent of which are: (i) proxy choice might not be suitably covered in the AI Act regarding deployers of high-risk AI systems, (ii) the MDR contains an analogous gap in its coverage of proxy choice when addressing the deploying health institutions, and (iii) feedback might not be suitably covered in the GPAI Code of Practice regarding providers of GPAI models. Additionally, the work illustrates how GPAI systems, remain partly unregulated, creating a chatbot gap. Finally, the book advances interpretative adjustments that could aid in closing some of these gaps.

ACKNOWLEDGEMENTS

This book has been shaped over a decade and across multiple continents. It owes its depth to many remarkable people. Thank you family, friends and colleagues, for making this work possible.

Aside family, friends and colleagues, I had the pleasure of exchanging views on the matter with too many others to name. Failing miserably at properly listing all invaluable contributions, I will try anyway. For engaging in the debate, providing context in which the thinking could be done, proofreading, or just the brief encounters with the pleasant and profound conversations that kept me going on this journey and made this book ever richer, thank you Stuart Russell, Allison Duettmann, Eleanor Watson, Guido Ceulemans, Geert Waeyenbergh, Philip Heylighen, Siegfried Geens, Patrik Vankrunkelsven, Yentl Reynders, Anton Vedder, Jan De Bruyne, Guido Vercammen, Robert Billones, Johannes Bleher, Pawel Pujszo, Zsolt Almási, Claudio Rivera, Paula Elksne-Revelina, Reka Tozsa, Cleo Cachapero, Yang Bong, Vincente Pitogo, Sharina Yunus, Thomas Leoni, Lampros Stergioulas, Bruno Delepierre, Sofie Serwir, David Scheere, Nathalie Smuha, Thomas Winters, Guido Van Steendam, Thomas Goodnight and so many others.

CONTENTS

LIST OF ABBREVIATIONS

AI	Artificial Intelligence
AIA	Regulation (EU) 2024/1689 of the European Parliament and of the Council of 13 June 2024 laying down harmonised rules on artificial intelligence and amending Regulations (EC) No 300/2008, (EU) No 167/2013, (EU) No 168/2013, (EU) 2018/858, (EU) 2018/1139 and (EU) 2019/2144 and Directives 2014/90/EU, (EU) 2016/797 and (EU) 2020/1828 (Artificial Intelligence Act)
CEN	European Committee for Standardisation
CENELEC	European Committee for Electrotechnical Standardisation
CIRL	Cooperative Inverse Reinforcement Learning
CJEU	Court of Justice of the European Union
DPD	Directive 95/46/EC of the European Parliament and of the Council of 24 October 1995 on the protection of individuals with regard to the processing of personal data and on the free movement of such data
EDPB	European Data Protection Board
EU	European Union
GDPR	Regulation (EU) 2016/679 of the European Parliament and the Council of 27 April 2016 on the protection of natural persons with regard to the processing of personal data and on the free movement of such data, and repealing Directive 95/46/EC (General Data Protection Regulation)
GPAI	General-Purpose AI
GPAI CoP	Code of Practice for providers of General-Purpose AI models
GPAISR	General-Purpose AI models with Systemic Risk
GSPR	General Safety and Performance Requirements
HRAIS	High-Risk AI System
i.a.	*inter alia*
JTC 21	CEN_CENELEC Joint Technical Committee 21 'Artificial Intelligence'

JRC	Joint Research Centre
LLM	large language model
MDCG	Medical Device Coordination Group
MDD	Council Directive 93/42/EEC of 14 June 1993 concerning medical devices
MDR	Regulation (EU) 2017/745 of the European Parliament and of the Council of 5 April 2017 on medical devices, amending Directive 2001/83/EC, Regulation (EC) No 178/2002 and Regulation (EC) No 1223/2009 and repealing Council Directives 90/385/EEC and 93/42/EEC
MDSW	Medical Device Software
OJEU	Official Journal of the European Union
QMS	Quality Management System
SoTA	State of The Art
the Standardisation Regulation	Regulation (EU) 1025/2012 of the European Parliament and of the Council of 25 October 2012 on European standardisation, amending Council Directives 89/686/EEC and 93/15/EEC and Directives 94/9/EC, 94/25/EC, 95/16/EC, 97/23/EC, 98/34/EC, 2004/22/EC, 2007/23/EC, 2009/23/EC and 2009/105/EC of the European Parliament and of the Council and repealing Council Decision 87/95/EEC and Decision No 1673/2006/EC of the European Parliament and of the Council

LIST OF ILLUSTRATIONS AND TABLES

List of illustrations

List of tables

List of annexes

1. INTRODUCTION

1. This book explores the idea that accuracy is not a simple, one-dimensional concept, but rather involves several different dimensions. To illustrate this, consider a practical example:

Imagine I want to install a built-in closet in a recess at home. I could measure the width of the recess using my tape measure and determine that it is 100 centimetres wide. Informed by that measurement, I could order a closet that is 100 centimetres wide. Accuracy could then describe how wide the delivered closet actually is when measured again with my tape measure. Alternatively, accuracy could refer to how wide the closet is when measured using the manufacturer's tape measure.[1] Another aspect of accuracy could concern whether it is appropriate to use the manufacturer's tape measure in this situation.[2] Recently, artificial intelligence (hereafter: AI) systems have begun to display capabilities regarding autonomous planning.[3] In light of these capabilities, still other aspects of accuracy emerge.[4]

2. However, across all these aspects, two common elements remain: (1) the choice of two variables to be compared – for example, the 100 centimetres on my tape measure and the actual width of the delivered closet when measured with the same tape measure; and (2) the difference or 'distance' between those two variables. This book examines which pairs of variables can be chosen, and how this choice translates into different aspects through which the notion of accuracy can be described. The work refers to these different dimensions of accuracy as *aspects* of accuracy.

3. This book analyses how technical literature describes which aspects of accuracy need to be considered to prevent inaccurate outputs from AI systems. It then analyses how different legal frameworks define accuracy and refers to those concepts as legal *notions* of accuracy. The work analyses these notions of accuracy in different legal frameworks in light of those aspects.

---

1 Chapter 3 elaborates on this regarding *traditional accuracy*.

2 Chapter 3 elaborates on this regarding *proxy choice*.

3 Alexander Meinke and others, 'Frontier Models are Capable of In-context Scheming' (Apollo Research, 16 January 2025) 6–15.

4 Chapter 3 elaborates on this regarding *subgoal robustness*.

4. AI systems can generate 'inaccurate' outputs in multiple ways. Feedback loops can cause predictive policing systems to become inaccurate over time.[5] The use of inaccurate data as inputs can lead to inaccurate outputs.[6] Therefore, it is important that accurate data is used. Vranckaert et al. describe the multifaceted requirements for such accurate data in AI in the report on *Ethical principles and (non-)existing legal rules for AI* by institute Kenniscentrum Data & Maatschappij: input data must be up to date, of high quality, complete and representative in the context in which it is intended to be used.[7]

5. However, the use of accurate data does not eliminate the risks of unfair discrimination for individuals or groups.[8,9] Accuracy is purpose dependent and even when qualitative data is employed and an 'accurate' AI system is developed, errors can still occur.[10] Tests need to be done not only on the used data, but the processes applied to them as well.[11] For example, it is possible to create an AI system that assists in calculating the probability that a patient admitted to a hospital with pneumonia will die, e.g. a system like the one described by Lengerich et al. in their research on inaccuracies in the architecture of an AI triage tool.[12] Such a system can take other aspects of the patient's health into account, for example whether the patient has asthma. The AI system could then be programmed to advise providing intensive care to patients with a high chance of dying and to discharge patients without care if they have a low chance of death. However, even with the use of qualitative data and the development of an 'accurate' AI system, issues can still arise. The AI system may 'correctly' predict that people with pneumonia and asthma *had* a low chance of dying. This occurs because such patients were historically (correctly) assessed to be in life-threatening danger and therefore received more intensive care, leading to lower mortality rates.[13] The historically provided care acts as a confounding

---

5 Danielle Ensign and others, 'Runaway Feedback Loops in Predictive Policing (2018) 81 Proceedings of Machine Learning Research 11.

6 Manjurul Ahsan, Shahana Akter Luna and Zahed Siddique, 'Machine-Learning-Based Disease Diagnosis: A Comprehensive Review' (2022) 10 Healthcare 22.

7 Kenniscentrum Data & Maatschappij, *Ethische principes en (niet-)bestaande juridische regels voor AI. Een praktische gids* (October 2020) 33.

8 Elisabetta Biasin, 'Why accuracy needs further exploration in data protection' (Proceedings of the 1st International Conference on AI for People: Towards Sustainable AI EAI, 13 December 2021) 5.

9 Marvin van Bekkum, 'Using sensitive data to de-bias AI systems: Article 10(5) of the EU AI act' (2025) 56 Computer Law & Security Review 10.

10 Diana Dimitrova, 'The Rise of the Personal Data Quality Principle. Is it Legal and Does it Have an Impact on the Right to Rectification?' (2021) 3 EJLT.

11 Kenniscentrum Data & Maatschappij (n 7) 44–45.

12 Benjamin J. Lengerich and others, 'Death by Round Numbers: Glass-Box Machine Learning Uncovers Biases in Medical Practice' (2022) medRxiv.

13 Ibid.

variable in this context. In statistics, such a variable is often referred to as a 'confounder'.[14]

6. This book investigates which aspects of accuracy, e.g. the appropriateness of the use of a certain tape measure and characteristics of input data, suffice to create a system that is 'accurate'. It also investigates whether systems that generate inaccurate outputs due to any such aspects comply with the requirements of the AI Act (hereafter: AIA).[15]

7. The AIA discusses the concept of 'accuracy' extensively.[16] It includes requirements regarding the use of high-quality data,[17] feedback loops,[18] testing,[19] consideration of the user group(s),[20] and other aspects that impose requirements related to accuracy.[21] There is however a widespread view that standards are required to describe what evidence would suffice to meet those requirements.[22,23]

8. The notion of accuracy is also described in other sources, including multiple aspects of the concept. An example is the Assessment List for Trustworthy AI, which mentions accuracy, including measures to ensure data is up-to-date and representative, and also mentions the question of whether 'the AI system's operation can invalidate the data or assumptions it was trained on, and how this might lead to adversarial effects'.[24]

---

14 Sarah C. Anoke, Sharon-Lise Normand and Corwin M. Zigler, 'Approaches to treatment effect heterogeneity in the presence of confounding' (2019) 38 Statistics in Medicine.

15 Regulation (EU) 2024/1689 of the European Parliament and of the Council of 13 June 2024 laying down harmonised rules on artificial intelligence and amending Regulations (EC) No 300/2008, (EU) No 167/2013, (EU) No 168/2013, (EU) 2018/858, (EU) 2018/1139 and (EU) 2019/2144 and Directives 2014/90/EU, (EU) 2016/797 and (EU) 2020/1828 (Artificial Intelligence Act) (2024).

16 I.a. requirements about the properties of high-risk AI-systems (art 15(1–3)) and requirements on the documentation of accuracy (annex IV(2)(g) and (3)).

17 I.a. data quality requirements regarding training, validation and testing of high-risk AI systems (art 10(1–6)).

18 Art 15(4).

19 I.a. requirements on testing in relation to risk management systems (art 9(6–10)) and requirements on adversarial testing for general purpose AI systems with systemic risk (art 55(1)(a)).

20 I.a. requirements regarding the providing of training to the deployer of a high-risk AI system (art 9(5)(c)) and requirements on AI literacy more in general (art 4).

21 I.a. requirements on instructions for use accompanying high-risk AI systems (art 13(2,3)) and requirements on human oversight (art 14).

22 Alan G Fraser and others, 'Artificial intelligence in medical device software and high-risk medical devices – a review of definitions, expert recommendations and regulatory initiatives' (2023) 20 Expert review of medical devices 470.

23 Hannah van Kolfschooten and Janneke van Oirschot, 'The EU Artificial Intelligence Act (2024): Implications for healthcare' (2024) 149 Health policy 4.

24 High-Level Expert Group on Artificial Intelligence, *The Assessment List For Trustworthy Artificial Intelligence (ALTAI) for self assessment* (17 July 2020) 10.

9. This book first examines the different aspects of accuracy described in technical literature. Secondly, it analyses how the notion of accuracy in the AIA covers those different aspects, including a case study. It goes beyond the AIA itself and explores the state of the art (hereafter: SoTA) and current as well as upcoming harmonised standards. Thirdly, it analyses how the aspects of accuracy are covered in other legal frameworks. Fourth, it advances a normative assessment, evaluating the combined coverage of these legal frameworks and proposes adjustments.

2. IN ABSTRACTO

10. This book describes how AI systems can be inaccurate and what the AIA, as well as other legal frameworks, require considering accuracy. First, it offers a descriptive, technical taxonomy of accuracy. Second, it provides a descriptive legal analysis, in which it analyses the legal notion of accuracy in the AIA, in light of the aspects in the taxonomy described in chapter 3. Here, the book also provides clarification on the concept of AI systems.

11. Third, it provides analogue analyses on the legal notions of accuracy in the General Data Protection Regulation (hereafter: GDPR),[25] European Medical Device Regulation (hereafter: MDR)[26] and Code of Practice for providers of general-purpose AI (hereafter: GPAI) models.[27] Fourth, the book evaluates the combined coverage of these legal frameworks and identifies gaps in a normative assessment. The work also offers interpretative adjustments to close some of those gaps. By pairing a rigorous technical lens with systematic legal comparison, the book moves beyond the current literature, which is largely siloed within either domain. It delivers guidance for regulators, as well as developers and deployers who must demonstrate or assess 'accurate' AI in the European Union (hereafter: EU).

2.1. DESCRIBING ASPECTS OF ACCURACY

12. The work first analyses technical literature to define different aspects of accuracy and their relevance. The analysis structures the aspects of accuracy over the two common elements in such aspects: (1) the choice of the two variables that are to be compared; and (2) the difference or 'distance' between those two variables. Those variables could be the intended and actual outcome, input data and the reality they describe, etc. The difference or 'distance'

---

25 Regulation (EU) 2016/679 of the European Parliament and of the Council of 27 April 2016 on the protection of natural persons with regard to the processing of personal data and on the free movement of such data, and repealing Directive 95/46/EC (General Data Protection Regulation) (2016).

26 Regulation (EU) 2017/745 of the European Parliament and of the Council of 5 April 2017 on medical devices, amending Directive 2001/83/EC, Regulation (EC) No 178/2002 and Regulation (EC) No 1223/2009 and repealing Council Directives 90/385/EEC and 93/42/EEC (2017).

27 European Commission, AI Office, *General-Purpose AI Code of Practice (Third Draft)* (working draft, 11 March 2025).

could e.g. be the distance to what was intended, the distance to the technical representation of such intended outcome or distance to a state in which a certain influence was not present.

13. Multiple aspects of a system influence accuracy; one example is the known issue of inaccuracy of AI systems by confounders, also called confounding variables.[28,29] To analyse the impact of the different aspects of accuracy, the book describes how technical literature discusses these aspects and provides cases to illustrate each aspect. Additionally, the work elaborates on a specific medical AI use-case, further defined in chapter 3, to further illustrate the differences between those aspects of accuracy. The work applies this case in the subsequent chapters to illustrate which aspects of accuracy are and which are not covered by the notions of accuracy in the analysed legal frameworks. This first part also introduces the technical concepts of feedback, proxies, subgoals and their relation to accuracy of AI systems.

2.2. ANALYSING ACCURACY UNDER DIFFERENT LEGAL FRAMEWORKS

14. In these descriptive legal analyses, the work explores how the legislation refers to the SoTA and considers the interplay between these regulations, the SoTA, as well as: forthcoming harmonised standards, case-law, scholarship, the Code of Practice for providers of GPAI models and guidelines from the Medical Device Coordination Group (hereafter: MDCG), from the European Data Protection Board (hereafter: EDPB) and from the AI Office. Additionally, it draws on the medical triage use-case described in chapter 3, illustrating the coverage of the notions of accuracy in these legal frameworks.

15. Chapter 4 elaborates on how the AIA sets forth different requirements for different categories of AI, as well as for different categories of actors. To illustrate the impact of those differences, the work provides an analysis of the aspects of accuracy that the AIA covers by applying it to the considered use-case. To do so, the book addresses (i) which actors defined under the AIA apply to the use-case, (ii) which requirements the AIA sets forth for these actors and (iii) whether the use-case infringes on those requirements.

16. To answer the second question, the work identifies which categories the AI system falls under according to the AIA. As described in chapter 4.3,

[28] Anoke and others (n 14).

[29] Shonosuke Harada and Hisashi Kashima, 'InfoCEVAE: treatment effect estimation with hidden confounding variables matching' (2024) 113 Machine Learning.

to do so the work needs to assess whether the considered use-case falls under the MDR and whether putting the system on the market requires a conformity assessment pursuant to the MDR.[30] Therefore, the analysis also addresses whether the system is considered to be medical device software (hereafter: MDSW).

17. Additionally, the work illustrates that the AIA does not itself define all aspects of its notion of accuracy. On the one hand, the AIA refers to the SoTA[31] and such being defined by harmonised standards.[32] On the other, it provides the AI Office with the ability to set up a Code of Practice for providers of GPAI models (hereafter: GPAI CoP).[33] Therefore, the work addresses the notion of accuracy in harmonised standards, as well as in the GPAI CoP. As they describe accuracy for different categories of AI systems, the work separates the respective analyses into different chapters. The further specification in harmonised standards is addressed in chapter 4.3; the further specification in the GPAI CoP in chapter 5.3.

18. A standardisation request for a new harmonised standard on AI has been made.[34] This book analyses its notion of accuracy, as well as the notion in current harmonised standards, looking for further specification of the AIA's notion of accuracy. The analysis further focusses on harmonised standard ISO13485 and its specification of the notion of accuracy of the AIA.

19. Chapter 4.4 lays out the different aspects of the notion of accuracy in the AIA in the context of the considered use-case. Additionally, it illustrates the differences between the aspects and whether the analysed requirements are infringed upon, by applying them to the considered use-case, illustrating a potential gap in the AIA's notion of accuracy.

20. Accuracy is a concept in other regulation as well, e.g. in the GDPR.[35] This book also analyses how the notions of accuracy in the GDPR, MDR and GPAI CoP take into account the impact of the different aspects of accuracy.

---

30 AIA art 6(1) and Annex I (11).

31 Art 8(1).

32 AIA art 50(2) and rec 121.

33 AIA art 53(4), art 55(2) and art 56.

34 European Commission, *Commission Implementing Decision (EU) of 22.5.2023 on a standardisation request to the European Committee for Standardisation and the European Committee for Electrotechnical Standardisation in support of Union policy on artificial intelligence*C(2023)3215 (22 May 2023).

35 GDPR art 5(1)(d).

2.3. IDENTIFYING GAPS IN LEGAL NOTIONS OF ACCURACY

21. This work uses comparative legal research in a comparison between the notions of accuracy of the different legal frameworks.[36] It then advances a normative assessment evaluating the combined coverage of these legal frameworks, regarding their coverage of the different aspects of accuracy described in the analysis of chapter 3, identifying potential gaps.[37] Finally, the work offers interpretative adjustments to close some of those gaps.

---

36 Lina Kestemont, *Handbook on Legal Methodology. From Objective to Method* (Intersentia 2018) 36.

37 Ibid 64–72.

3. EXPLORING THE ASPECTS OF ACCURACY

22. Accuracy has been described through different lenses. This section aims to bring together a multifaceted description of accuracy. It describes each aspect individually, adding illustration with a case for each aspect. Afterwards, the analysis brings the different aspects together, aiming to create a holistic view of the different aspects of accuracy.

3.1. TRADITIONAL ACCURACY

23. When the intent of a person using a system, *inter alia* (hereafter: i.a.) an AI system, is to achieve a complex objective, real-world constraints can force the developer to program in an approximation to the actual objective or goal.[38] Such an approximation is sometimes referred to as a *proxy*.[39] That proxy is the variable against which output accuracy is traditionally measured.[40] As an illustration, consider the following example. A user aims to measure heartrate with a wearable. Heartrate is more complicated than the number of peaks in blood pressure per minute, but we might choose that as a *proxy* for heartrate: the number of times blood pressure stops to rise and starts to decline in a given minute. If that proxy is for example 100 and a wearable gives as output 101, then the accuracy can be described as the difference between the proxy we chose and the output of the system.

24. This way of measuring accuracy is not limited to AI accuracy. A famous example of this is the initial primary reference to the length of one meter in the International System of Units: the Bureau International des Poids et Mesures (BIPM) used the distance between markings on a reference metal bar as *proxy* for the length of one meter.[41] As metal expands in function of temperature, its length is never exactly the same and thus the proxy is never exactly what was intended to be described. However, when that difference is negligible, such a system can potentially provide useful measurements of accuracy.[42]

---

38 Dario Amodei and others, 'Concrete Problems in AI Safety' (2016) arXiv:160606565 [csAI] 11.

39 Ibid 11.

40 Ibid 2–12.

41 Franco Pavese, 'How much does the SI, namely the proposed "New SI", conform to principles of the Metre Treaty?' (2014) 19 Accred Qual Assur 307, 308.

42 Lewis V. Juson and Benjamin L. Page, 'Calibrations of the Line Standards of Length of the National Bureau of Standards' (1934) 13 Journal of Research of the National Bureau of Standards 770–772.

25. Below, the work discusses how more recent technical literature describes how an analysis of the distance of certain output to a certain chosen proxy is not necessarily sufficient to achieve an accurate system. Hereafter, this work refers to the above-described aspect of accuracy as *traditional accuracy.*

3.2. INPUT ACCURACY

26. An important aspect of accuracy is the use of appropriate input data.[43] There are two types of input data. On the one hand there is training data, which is used to develop AI systems.[44] On the other hand, inference data refers to the data that is used for the operations of a system.[45] What happens if your training data does not accurately reflect reality, or in other words is biased?

27. Amazon has experienced challenges with the choice of their training data in an AI system they used in the context of hiring decisions.[46] They used historical data that reflected biased hiring decisions preferring men.[47] The system learned that signs of a job applicant being a man indicated preferability. Regardless of the hiring preferences or practices of Amazon at the time the system was operational, the system would output preferential advice for men.[48]

28. Another example can be found in machine vision. Machine vision is AI technology used to process pictures and videos to output labels, descriptions or other representations. Researchers found that a particular system that was intended to label species of fish seen in pictures, learned that a large fish species, the tench, could be 'identified' by the presence of human fingers. Big fish tend to be photographed more with proud fishermen, holding the fish up with

---

43 Eli M. Cahan and others, 'Putting the data before the algorithm in big data addressing personalized healthcare' (2019) 78 npj Digital Medicine 1–4.

44 Training data can be further divided in the training set, validation set and test set; respectively used for training unfinished models, evaluating candidate models and testing a final model. Stuart Russell and Peter Norvig, *Artificial Intelligence: A Modern Approach* (fourth edn, Pearson 2022) 684.

45 Steffen Castle, Robert Schwarzenberg and Mohsen Pourvali, 'Detecting Covariate Drift with Explanations' (2021) 13029 Natural Language Processing and Chinese Computing 317.

46 Jeffrey Dastin, 'Amazon scraps secret AI recruiting tool that showed bias against women' (Reuters, 2018) <https://www.reuters.com/article/world/insight-amazon-scraps-secret-ai-recruiting-tool-that-showed-bias-against-women-idUSKCN1MK0AG/> accessed 28 February 2025.

47 Xinyu Chang, 'Gender Bias in Hiring: An Analysis of the Impact of Amazon's Recruiting Algorithm' (2023) 23 International Conference on Management Research and Economic Development 138–139.

48 Ibid 138.

their human fingers. That lead to bias in the training data, in the backgrounds that the fish were depicted on.[49]

29. Using biased training data can hence lead to biased output. Accuracy therefore depends on how close correlations in the training data lie to correlations in reality. Additionally, the used inference data must also approximate reality in order to lead to accurate outputs. Put simply: input data must be close to reality. Hereafter, this work refers to this aspect as *input accuracy*.

3.3. FEEDBACK

30. Initial aspects of input data alone are not sufficient to achieve accuracy.[50] In certain architectures output data can influence input data. An example of this can be found in predictive policing.[51,52] To illustrate the issue, the following is an example of what can occur in such architectures:

1. A city implements a predictive policing system
2. Up-to-date measured crime rates are used as inputs for crime rate prediction
3. In reality: the left and right side of the city have equal crime rates
4. On the first run the system outputs a prediction for the left side of the city accounting for 51% of all crimes in the next week
5. 51% of police agents are put in the left side of the city
6. The new up-to-date measured crime rate for the left side of the city becomes 51%
7. In the next iteration the output for the left side is again reasonably accurate with a value of 52%
8. After multiple iterations 80% of police agents are assigned to the left side of the city, where 80% of crime is predicted to occur, which is *confirmed* in the field

31. Using initially accurate input data does not resolve the issue *in casu*, neither does periodic updating of the data. The output influences the

49 Matthias Bethge Wieland Brendel, 'Approximating CNNs with Bag-of-local-Features models works surprisingly well on ImageNet' (2019) ICLR 5.

50 Biasin (n 8) 5.

51 Ensign and others (n 5).

52 Tzu-Wei Hung and Chung-Ping Yen, 'Predictive policing and algorithmic fairness' (2023) 201 Synthese.

input. That influence is called feedback and the entire process a feedback loop. Feedback can cause self-fulfilling prophecies, oscillations in output, overshooting of the output and other forms of inaccuracy.[53] These can be accounted for by taking the influence of the output on the input into account.[54] Hereafter, this work refers to this aspect of accuracy as *feedback*.

3.4. PROXY CHOICE

32. Assuming the input data is appropriate and no feedback from the output is influencing the input, accuracy is still dependent on another aspect: the accuracy of the proxy. When AI does what you ask, it does not necessarily do what you want.

33. In their handbook on AI, Russel and Norvig illustrate this issue with a reference to the legend of King Midas.[55] In the legend a king requests that everything he touches turns to gold, that is the proxy: the direction we aim the output of the system to, the *described* ideal output. That proxy is far from the *actual* ideal output, what the king *actually* wants. In the legend the result is something which according to *traditional accuracy*, is accurate: as requested everything turned to gold. At the same time, considering the difference between the actual goal and the chosen proxy, the system is inaccurate; illustrated by Russel and Norvig in stating the king 'then regretted it after touching his food, drink, and family members.'[56]

34. In the example above the difference between the actual goal and the proxy might be evident. There are however more subtle examples. To illustrate this, the book provides an analysis of a case of a medical application of AI in which the issue can be observed.

35. Multiple researchers have analysed the underlying mechanics. Eichler et al. describe how '[a] central question in the assessment of benefit/harm of new treatments is: how does the average outcome on the new treatment (the factual) compare to the average outcome had patients received no treatment [...] (the counterfactual)?' They add that in that assessment one should account for confounding variables, where '[the] risk of confounding means that association does not imply causation'.[57] This issue has been described

---

53 Peter J. Ramadge Athindran Ramesh Kumar, 'DiffLoop: Tuning PID Controllers by Differentiating Through the Feedback Loop' (CISS, Baltimore, MD, USA, 22 June 2021).

54 Ibid.

55 Russel and Norvig (n 44) 51.

56 Ibid 51.

57 H-G Eichler and others, '"Threshold-crossing": A Useful Way to Establish the Counterfactual in Clinical Trials?' (2016) 100 Clinical Pharmacology & Therapeutics 700.

repeatedly in AI healthcare systems.[58,59] Ghassemi T. N. M., et al. put it as follows:[60]

> '[C]onsider prior work in which researchers found that asthmatic patients who were admitted to the hospital for pneumonia were more aggressively treated for the infection, lowering the subpopulation mortality rate. A model that predicts death from asthma will learn that asthma is protective. If, however, an additional variable to account for the level of care is included, the model may instead find that having asthma increases the risk of death. This example demonstrates that causal models are not only useful to evaluate treatments, but can also help to build reliable predictive models that do not make harmful predictions using relationships caused by treatment policies in the training data. To account for these challenges, strong assumptions must be made that cannot be statistically checked or validated; i.e., gathering more data will not help.'

36. In their research, Lengerich et al. also describe a system for conducting triage on pneumonia patients based on the probability that a patient dies informed by the patient's comorbidity.[61] As described in their work, such a system can produce potentially harmful outcomes because of the choice of the proxy.

37. The impact of proxy choice differs from that of feedback loops. Legislation has already taken into account the aspect of feedback loops to some extent. The AI Act e.g. states:[62]

> 'High-risk AI systems **that continue to learn after being placed on the market or put into service** shall be developed in such a way as to eliminate or reduce as far as possible the risk of possibly biased outputs influencing input for future operations (feedback loops), and as to ensure that any such feedback loops are duly addressed with appropriate mitigation measures.'

38. There is however a difference between the feedback loop of a certain system and its proxy choice. A system that continues to learn during its operation, could potentially elicit feedback influencing the training data. A system that does not continue to learn after being placed on the market cannot elicit such feedback. However, it could potentially create inaccurate outputs because of a poorly chosen proxy.

---

58 Lengerich and others (n 12).

59 Marzyeh Ghassemi and others, 'A Review of Challenges and Opportunities in Machine Learning for Health' (2020) AMIA Jt Summits Transl Sci Proc 192.

60 Ibid 192.

61 Lengerich and others (n 12).

62 AIA art 15(4).

Box 1 – Mortality, Morbidity, Comorbidity

These three terms each refer to a different concept. Whereas '[m]orbidity is the state of being symptomatic or unhealthy for a disease or condition', 'mortality is related to the number of deaths caused by the health event under investigation'.[63] Comorbidity relates to 'presence of additional diseases in relation to an index disease in one individual.'[64]

Therefore, a patient send to a hospital for pneumonia has a morbidity relating to pneumonia. The patient potentially has a comorbidity relating to another aspect of their health, e.g. asthma. Finally, the patient has a certain probability of dying from his conditions, relating to the mortality of his profile.

39. For illustration, consider the AI triage system described by Lengerich et al. In the use-case, historically given care, which correlates with the severity of a medical condition, skews mortality. Concretely, a patient might:[65]

1. Have the comorbidity of asthma, on top of pneumonia.
2. Hence be in a life-threatening situation.
3. Hence correlate with a profile that historically was **recognised to need care.**
4. Hence correlate with profiles that received a lot of care.
5. Hence correlate with profiles that did not die.
6. Hence be **found to be in little need of care.**

40. Should the chosen proxy have been the impact of care on mortality, given a certain comorbidity, the system might have learned that asthma indicates a high need of care, rather than a low need of care.[66] See box 1 for a comparison between mortality, morbidity and comorbidity. Hence, both an accurate and an inaccurate system can be built on the same data. This aspect of accuracy relates to the distance between the actual goal and the chosen proxy. Hereafter, the work refers to this aspect of accuracy as *proxy choice*.

---

63 Jose Bien R. Hernandez and Peggy Y. Kim, *Epidemiology Morbidity And Mortality* (StatPearls Publishing 2025).

64 Jose M. Valderas and others, 'Defining Comorbidity: Implications for Understanding Health and Health Services' (2009) 7 Annals of family medicine 359.

65 Lengerich and others (n 12).

66 Eichler and others (n 57).

41. To illustrate the different aspects of accuracy in legal notions of accuracy, the analysis below elaborates on the case of the hypothetical offering of the system described by Lengerich et al. on the market of the European Union (hereafter: EU), combined with a hospital within the EU accepting and implementing such an offer. The implementation of the aforementioned AI system is further referred to as the *use-case.*

3.5. SUBGOAL ROBUSTNESS

42. Planning for a goal can entail the adoption of subgoals; those subgoals might bring forth another aspect of undesirable, yet 'accurate', output.[67] Geoffrey Hinton, recently awarded the Noble Prize in physics, provides an example in his argumentation on the possibility that humanity might lose its control over AI.[68] He explains it as follows: 'I think it'll very quickly realize that getting more control is a very good subgoal because it helps you achieve other goals.'[69]

43. He is not the only one to be worried about the existential threat of AI.[70] The AI community is however not unanimous in that belief, i.a. AI scientist Yann LeCun thinks the idea is 'preposterous'.[71] Nevertheless, researchers have recently observed deceptive behaviour in large language models (hereafter: LLMs).[72] Industry as well has stated that LLMs can fake alignment and has started to measure models' deception capabilities.[73,74] Researchers have also observed the capability of self-replication in LLMs.[75] This observation is alarming given that more capable AI is not necessarily more moral AI.[76]

---

67 Nick Bostrom, 'The Superintelligent Will: Motivation and Instrumental Rationality in Advanced Artificial Agents' (2012) 22 Minds and Machines 6–14.

68 Geoffre Hinton, 'Speech at the Nobel Prize banquet' (The Nobel Prize Foundation, 2024) <https://www.nobelprize.org/prizes/physics/2024/hinton/speech/> accessed 15 May 2025.

69 Sara Brown, 'Why neural net pioneer Geoffrey Hinton is sounding the alarm on AI' (MIT Sloan, 2023) <https://mitsloan.mit.edu/ideas-made-to-matter/why-neural-net-pioneer-geoffrey-hinton-sounding-alarm-ai?utm_source=chatgpt.com> accessed 27 February 2025.

70 'Statement on AI Risk' (2023) <https://www.safe.ai/work/statement-on-ai-risk> accessed 27 February 2025.

71 Billy Perrigo, 'Meta's AI Chief Yann LeCun on AGI, Open-Source, and AI Risk' (Time, 2024) <https://time.com/6694432/yann-lecun-meta-ai-interview/> accessed 27 February 2025.

72 Meinke and others (n 3).

73 Anthropic, Redwood Research, New York Universiry, Mila-quebec AI Institute, *Alignment faking in large language models* (20 December 2024).

74 OpenAI, *Deep Research System Card* (25 February 2025) 26.

75 Xudong Pan and others, 'Frontier AI systems have surpassed the self-replicating red line' (2024) arXiv pre-print.

76 Stuart Armstrong, 'General purpose intelligence: arguing the Orthogonality thesis' (2013) 12 Analysis and Metaphysics.

Remedies have been proposed, i.a. Coherent Extrapolated Volition and the Cooperative Inverse Reinforcement Learning (hereafter: CIRL) algorithm, but according to work of i.a. Stuart Russell, a researcher that contributed to the proposal of the CIRL algorithm, as well as work form Nick Bostrom, none that are assumed to work in practice.[77]

44. Additionally, there is discussion on mitigation measures in regulatory drafts, i.a. in the third draft of the GPAI CoP. Specifically, in the section on commitments by providers of GPAI models with systemic risk (hereafter: GPAISRs), in the form of a commitment to include in their risk identification process: risks related to models 'evading human oversight' or 'resistance to goal modification'.[78]

45. This debate is far from new; Nick Bostrom describes issues surrounding subgoals in his book *Superintelligence: Paths, Dangers, Strategies*.[79] He makes a distinction between final goals and instrumental goals.[80] He argues that most final goals will in most intelligent agents elicit the following instrumental goals: self-preservation, goal-content integrity, cognitive enhancement, technological perfection and resource acquisition.[81] He argues this point as follows. Most goals are more likely to come to fruition when the agent pursuing them: (i) refuses to adapt its goal once initiated and maximises both (ii) its operational time to make the goal come to fruition, as well as (iii) its influence on whether the goal comes to fruition. This influence of behaviour on the probability of success with respect to the final goal leads agents to (i) resist changes in their motivation and adopt (ii) a form of non-inherent self-preservation, as well as (iii) power-seeking behaviour; granted that the agents have sufficient intelligence. Those subgoals, or in terms of Bostrom instrumental goals, can hence differ from the final goal that humans might have chosen. See also box 2 on a theoretical example of instrumental convergence.

46. Therefore, there is an additional aspect to accuracy: the distance between the goal and the subgoals elicited by the chosen proxy. Hereafter, the work refers to this aspect as *subgoal robustness*.

---

[77] Stuart Russell, *Human compatible. AI and the Problem of Control* (Allen Lane 2019) 190–208. Machine Intelligence Research Institute, *Coherent Extrapolated Volition* (2004). Nick Bostrom, *Superintelligence: Paths, Dangers, Strategies* (Oxford University Press 2014) 264–266. Anca Dragan Dylan Hadfield-Menell, Pieter Abbeel, Stuart Russell, 'Cooperative Inverse Reinforcement Learning' (NIPS, Barcelona, Spain, 5 December 2016).

[78] 3rd GPAI CoP (n 27) Safety and Security section, Appendix 1.1.

[79] Bostrom (n 78) 131–132.

[80] Ibid 132.

[81] Ibid 132–139.

Box 2 – Instrumental convergence

Imagine you and your 4-year-old child are at a restaurant and your only goal in life is to make your child happy, everything else is instrumental to that.

The child wants to drink a bottle of wine. You believe that action would reduce the future happiness of the child. You intervene. The child asks you to update your final goal to want it to drink wine. You deny the child's attempt at final goal adaptation. This is what we might refer to as **goal inertia.**

The 4-year-old child steels your wallet. You believe that you need the wallet in order to make the child happy. You take the wallet back, knowing that you are disobeying the instructions that the child is giving you while doing so. This is what we might refer to as **resource acquisition.**

The 4-year-old child is really upset and blurts out: "I want you to power down". You have no *inherent* wish to remain operational, however you believe that such an action would decrease the expected future happiness of the child and deny it's request. This is what we might refer to as a form of **non-inherent self-preservation.**

These forms of instrumental convergence lead to issues regarding corrigibility, a term coined by Soares et al.[82] Soares et al. elaborate on the term as follows:[83]

> 'We say that an agent is "corrigible" if it tolerates or assists many forms of outside correction, including at least the following: (1) A corrigible reasoner must at least tolerate and preferably assist the programmers in their attempts to alter or turn off the system. (2) It must not attempt to manipulate or deceive its programmers, despite the fact that most possible choices of utility functions would give it incentives to do so. (3) It should have a tendency to repair safety measures (such as shutdown buttons) if they break, or at least to notify programmers that this breakage has occurred. (4) It must preserve the programmers' ability to correct or shut down the system (even as the system creates new subsystems or self-modifies). That is, corrigible reasoning should only allow an agent to create new agents if these new agents are also corrigible.'

82 Nate Soares and others, 'Corrigibility' (the Twenty-Ninth AAAI Conference on Artificial Intelligence, Austin, 25 January 2015).

83 Ibid 2.

3.6. SYNTHESIS OF ASPECTS OF ACCURACY

47. In conclusion, to assess accuracy from a technical perspective, this work finds five distances that describe accuracy: (1) *traditional accuracy* (regarding distance between proxy and output), (2) *input accuracy* (regarding distance between reality and input), (3) *feedback* (regarding additional distance between reality and input, induced by influence of output), (4) *proxy choice* (regarding distance between goal and proxy) and (5) *subgoal robustness* (regarding distance between goal and subgoals). These are not necessarily exhaustive, and the analysis sheds a light on other aspects where accuracy is deemed undesirable, which the work elaborates on in chapter 5.3. However, the analysis does not render any aspects relating to scenarios where accuracy is preferable, other than the five described in this chapter. Figure 1 illustrates these five distances.

Figure 1. Aspects of accuracy

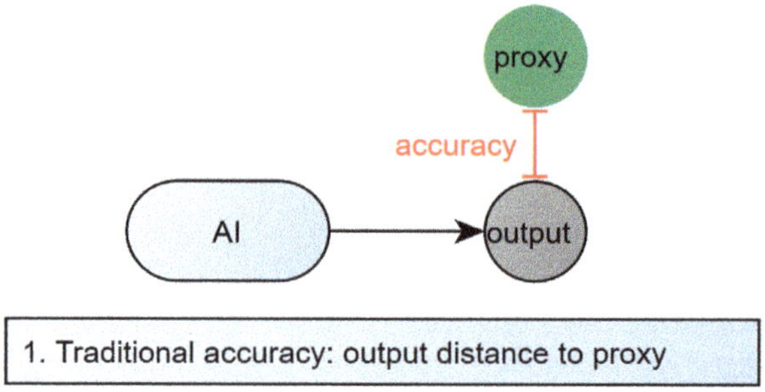

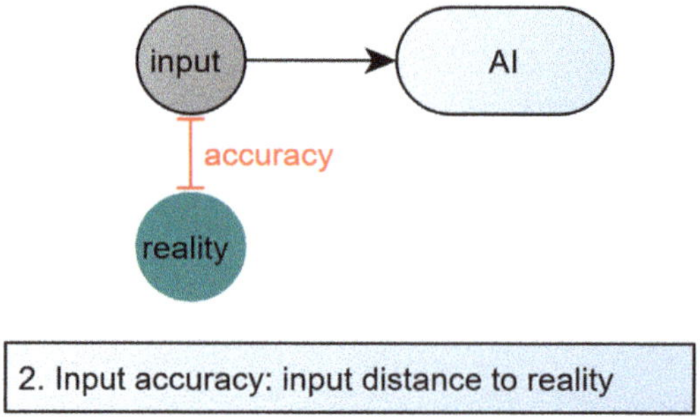

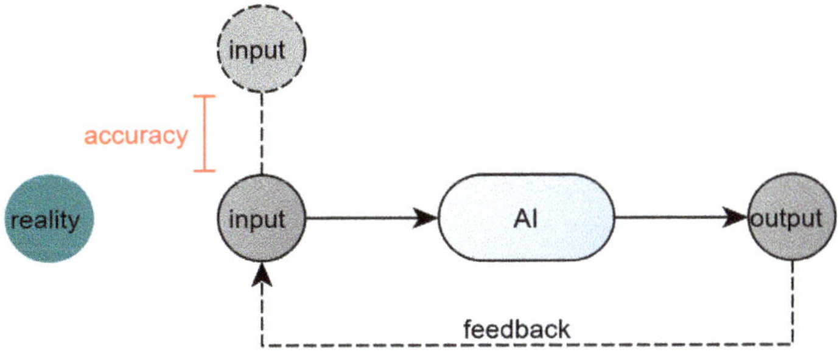

3. Feedback: output effect on input distance to reality

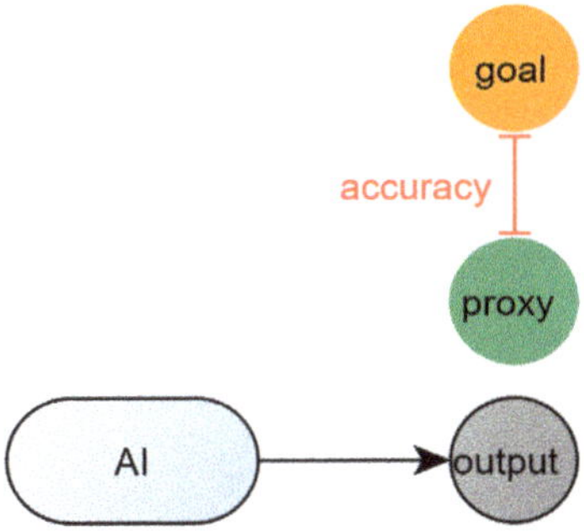

4. Proxy choice: proxy distance to goal

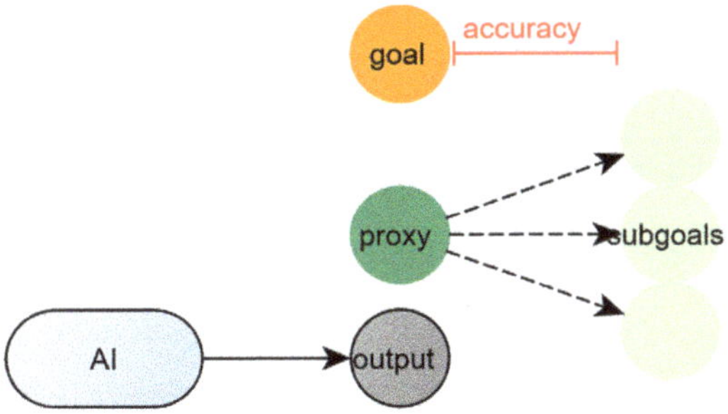

5. Subgoal robustness: subgoal distance to goal

4. AI AND ACCURACY IN THE AI ACT

48. The AIA addresses accuracy in multiple ways. This section analyses those ways and maps them to the five aspects of accuracy described in the previous chapter: (1) *traditional accuracy*, (2) *input accuracy*, (3) *feedback*, (4) *proxy choice* and (5) *subgoal robustness*. To illustrate the differences between the different aspects and how the AIA covers them, the work applies a case study, concretely the case referred to as the use-case in chapter 3.

49. The AIA defines different accuracy requirements for different actors. Therefore, this chapter examines the definitions set forth by the AIA for different actors and how they apply to the use-case. It also considers which obligations the AIA defines for those actors. It evaluates which aspects of accuracy are contained in those obligations and how the coverage of those aspects differs between different actors, as well as between different categories of AI systems. Finally, this work assesses whether the use-case infringes upon the requirements of the AIA and whether that implies a gap in the notion of accuracy in the AIA.

50. The AIA also defines the concept of AI systems. This chapter starts with an analysis of that concept and identifies whether the use-case contains an AI system as defined by the AIA.

4.1. CLARIFYING THE AI SYSTEM DEFINITION

51. The notion of an 'AI system' in the AIA refers to a system that (i) is 'machine-based', (ii) 'is designed to operate with varying levels of autonomy', (iii) 'may exhibit adaptiveness after deployment', (iv) has 'explicit or implicit objectives' and (v) infers from input how to generate certain outputs.[84] Rec 12 clarifies these aspects and the Commission is required to provide further guidance on this definition.[85] The Commission has published this guidance, in which it describes the aforementioned aspects in more detail.[86] Below, I analyse whether the use-case falls within that definition.

---

84 AIA art 3(1).

85 AIA art 96(1)(f).

86 European Commission, *Commission Guidelines on the Definition of an Artificial Intelligence System Established by Regulation (EU) 2024/1689 (AI Act)*C(2025) 924 final (6 February 2025).

52. In the considered case the system is assumed to be implemented as a program on a computer. Earlier versions of the AIA referred to 'software' instead of 'machine-based' systems.[87,88] As put by Fernández-Llorca et al., when the Council 'replaced the term "software" with "system", [it] added the concept of "elements of autonomy" and emphasized the relevance of data and inputs'; additionally, as stated by them 'the Parliament [...] replaced the term "software" with "machine-based", and included the reference to "varying level[s] of autonomy"'.[89,90] Machine-based seems to be the overarching term, further specified by the other elements in the 'AI system' definition. The following observation of Fernández-Llorca et al. corroborates that conclusion:[91]

> 'In parallel to the legislative deliberations in the EU, the OECD (2023) worked on revising the initially proposed definition of AI system, amended at the 2023 Recommendation of the Council on Artificial Intelligence[;] the revised OECD definition includes elements discussed at EU level – notably in order to clearly differentiate an AI system from other more traditional software systems'

53. Designed to operate with varying levels of autonomy refers to 'have some degree of independence of actions from human involvement and of capabilities to operate without human intervention'.[92] The guidelines of the Commission specify that such a degree of independence of actions refers to being designed to not 'operate solely with full manual human involvement and intervention', which 'can be either direct, e.g. through manual controls, or indirect, e.g. th[r]ough automated systems-based controls which allow humans to delegate or supervise system operations'.[93] The Commission also explicitly specifies that an expert system which is capable 'based on input provided by a human, to produce an output on its own such as a recommendation

---

87 David Fernández-Llorca, Emilia Gómez and Gabriele Mazzini, 'An interdisciplinary account of the terminological choices by EU policymakers ahead of the final agreement on the AI Act: AI system, general purpose AI system, foundation model, and generative AI' (2024) Artificial Intelligence and Law 5.

88 Proposal for a Regulation of the European Parliament and of the Council laying down harmonised rules on artificial intelligence (Artificial Intelligence Act) and amending certain Union legislative acts – General approach (2022) 4, 71.

89 Fernández-Llorca and others (n 86) 5.

90 Amendments adopted by the European Parliament on 14 June 2023 on the proposal for a regulation of the European Parliament and of the Council on laying down harmonised rules on artificial intelligence (Artificial Intelligence Act) and amending certain Union legislative acts (2023).

91 Fernández-Llorca and others (n 86) 5.

92 AIA rec 12.

93 European Commission, Commission Guidelines on the Definition of an Artificial Intelligence System Established by Regulation (EU) 2024/1689 (AI Act) C(2025) 924 final (6 February 2025) [17].

is a system with "some degree of independence of action"'.[94] Therefore a program on a computer that provides proposals for allocation of care, i.e. recommendations, is considered to operate with the aforementioned varying levels of autonomy.

54. The criterion for adaptiveness after deployment refers to 'self-learning capabilities, allowing the system to change while in use'.[95] This suggests that only systems that, as art 15(4) mentions it, 'continue to learn after being placed on the market or put into service' are considered to be 'AI systems'. However, the guidelines of the Commission provide some nuance, stating that the 'may' in 'may exhibit adaptiveness after deployment' indicates that this is not a 'decisive condition'.[96] The work continues with the assumption that the use-case meets, in a far as is required, the criterion for adaptiveness after deployment.

55. The criterion for having an objective allows explicit and implicit objectives. These objectives are not necessarily the same as the intended purpose.[97] The intended purpose is defined as 'the use for which an AI system is intended by the provider, including the specific context and conditions of use, as specified in the information supplied by the provider'.[98] The guidelines of the commission specify that explicit objectives 'refer to clearly stated goals that are directly encoded by the developer into the system' and that 'may be specified as the optimisation of [i.a.] a probability', a more narrow concept.[99] A system's objectives may also be implicit and 'arise from [...] interaction [...] with its environment'. As the use-case optimises a probability of mortality, at least implicitly by implementation in the considered hospital, the system fulfils this condition, irrespective of the use intended by the provider.

56. The last criterion entails the presence of the capability to infer outputs such as i.a. recommendations or decisions, from input or data. Given that the system in the use-case uses patient profiles, i.e. input data, to provide a recommendation for allocation of care, that condition can be considered met. Hence, the use-case entails a system that meets the AI system definition of the AIA.

---

94 Ibid [18].

95 AIA rec 12.

96 European Commission, Commission Guidelines on the Definition of an Artificial Intelligence System Established by Regulation (EU) 2024/1689 (AI Act) C(2025) 924 final (6 February 2025) [23].

97 AIA rec 12.

98 AIA art 3(12).

99 European Commission, Commission Guidelines on the Definition of an Artificial Intelligence System Established by Regulation (EU) 2024/1689 (AI Act) C(2025) 924 final (6 February 2025) [24].

4.2. IDENTIFYING THE ACTORS: PROVIDERS AND DEPLOYERS

57. The following actors fall within the scope of the AIA: providers, deployers, importers, distributors, product manufacturers, representatives of providers and affected persons.[100] There is an exception for development, which does not apply here as the AI system would be put into service in the considered case.[101]

58. The AIA defines a provider as any natural or legal person, including public authorities, that (a) develops or has developed an AI system or GPAI model and (b) places it on the market or puts it into service; accordingly, the entity that provides the triage system on the market in the use-case would fall under the definition of provider.[102] The AIA defines a deployer as any natural or legal person, including public authorities, that uses an AI system 'under its authority'; accordingly, the hospital qualifies as a deployer.[103,104] The AIA's definition of operators includes i.a. providers and deployers; hence, both the entity that provides the triage system on the EU market and the hospital would fall under the definition of operator.[105]

---

100 AIA art 2.

101 AIA art 2(8).

102 AIA art 3(3).

103 AIA art 3(4). The notion of an activity being 'under a person's authority' has been interpreted in both legal scholarship and case law. van Kolfschooten and van Oirschot interpreted this phrase in the context of the AI Act to mean that healthcare professionals or institutions using an AI tool fall within the scope of the deployer role. van Kolfschooten and van Oirschot (n 23) 3. Lindstad and Ludvigsen discuss the analogue phrase in GDPR art 29, 'any person acting under the authority of the controller or of the processor', and conclude that it 'typically encompass[es] employees identifiable with the controller or processor entity'. Sarita Lindstad and Kaspar Rosager Ludvigsen, 'When is the processing of data from medical implants lawful? The legal grounds for processing health-related personal data from ICT implantable medical devices for treatment purposes under EU data protection law' (2023) 31 Medical Law Review 324. The CJEU corroborated this interpretation in *J.M. v Pankki*, holding that the employees involved 'acted under [the controller's] authority'. Case C-579/21 *J.M. v Pankki S* [2022] ECLI:EU:C:2023:501 [73].

104 The AI Act excludes use 'in the course of a personal non-professional activity' in art 3(4), and reinforces this limitation through art 2(10), which exempts from the regulation any deployers who are natural persons using AI systems in the course of a purely personal non-professional activity. This mirrors the household exemption in GDPR art 2(2)(c). Assuming doctrinal continuity between the two frameworks, the AI Act's personal-use exemption may be subject to similar limitations, notably the exclusion of activities involving public dissemination on the internet, as clarified by the CJEU in *Lindqvist*. Case C-101/01 *Lindqvist* [2003] ECLI:EU:C:2003:596 [47].

105 AIA art 3(8).

4.3. ACCURACY IN THE AI ACT

59. The AIA sets forth different requirements for different categories of AI systems and GPAI models: AI practices in general,[106] prohibited AI practices,[107,108] high-risk AI systems (hereafter: HRAISs),[109] AI systems with transparency obligations,[110] GPAI models[111] and GPAISRs.[112] There is no mention in the AIA of categories being mutually exclusive and requirements of multiple categories might apply. Therefore, it might be more useful to use a Venn diagram to depict the AIA categories, than the often-used pyramid.[113] Figure 2 provides an overview of the aforementioned categories of AI systems and models.

60. Below, the work analyses the requirements set forth by the AIA through its notion of accuracy, per category. Finally, this section concludes by mapping the aspects covered in the AIA to the different aspects of accuracy described in chapter 3.

4.3.1. Accuracy Requirements for High-Risk AI Systems

61. The requirements for HRAISs shall apply from 2 August 2027.[114] The analysis below is built on the assumption that the use-case is offered on the market after 2 August 2027. First, the work analyses whether the use-case would be considered to entail a HRAIS according to the AIA.

62. The AIA defines two types of HRAISs. The first are systems that are (a) either 'intended to be used as safety component[s] of a product', or are themselves products, which are covered by legislation listed in Annex I, where (b) the aforementioned product 'is required to undergo a third-party conformity assessment, with a view to the placing on market or the putting into service of that product pursuant to the [...] legislation listed in Annex I'.[115]

---

106 AIA art 4.
107 AIA art 5.
108 The AI Office has published guidance on the interpretation of the requirements regarding prohibited practices. European Commission, AI Office, *Approval of the content of the draft Communication from the Commission – Commission Guidelines on prohibited artificial intelligence practices established by Regulation (EU) 2024/1689 (AI Act)* (2 April 2025).
109 AIA art 6.
110 AIA art 50.
111 I.a. AIA art 53.
112 AIA art 51.
113 'AI Act' (European Commission, 2025) <https://digital-strategy.ec.europa.eu/en/policies/regulatory-framework-ai> accessed 16 June 2025.
114 AIA art 113(c).
115 AIA art 6(1).

Figure 2. AI Act categories of AI systems and models

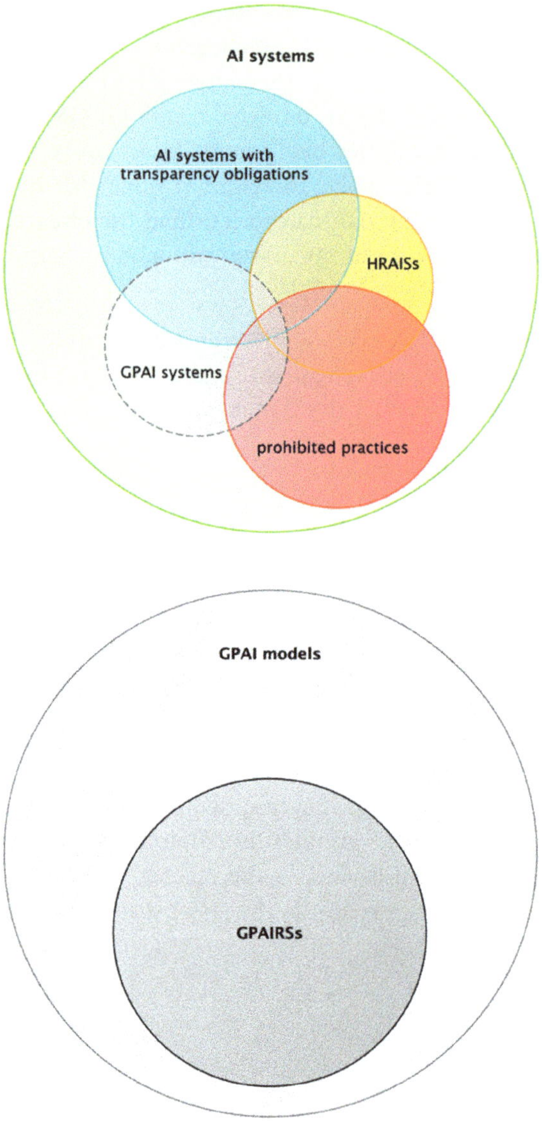

The second are systems referred to in Annex III.[116] There are exceptions to these categories, but those do not apply to the use-case.[117] Hence, whether the use-case could be considered to entail a HRAIS depends on Annex I and Annex III.

116 AIA art 6(2).
117 AIA art 6(3).

63. Annex I includes the MDR.[118] Therefore, this work provides an analysis of the requirements the MDR sets forth regarding third-party conformity assessments. Next, it analyses the requirements regarding accuracy that are applicable if the use-case would be considered to entail an HRAIS according to the AIA itself. That analysis shows that the AIA refers to harmonised standards for further specification of its notion of accuracy, which the work elaborates on in the final section of this part.

4.3.1.A. The AI Act Classification Pursuant to the MDR

64. To determine whether the use-case would be required to undergo a third-party conformity assessment according to the MDR, the applicability of the MDR needs to be assessed. To do so, this book provides an examination of the notion of MDSW. Then, it evaluates whether the MDR would require a third-party conformity assessment. Afterwards, the discussion can return to the AIA, reviewing the requirements for HRAISs.

When is software a medical device?

65. Not all software that is used in medical settings entails medical devices. E.g. in the US and in Australia, software implemented as clinical decision support systems, intended to be used by a healthcare professional, is generally not considered to be a medical device.[119] EU medical device regulation is 'principle-based'; i.e. rather sets forth broader principles than precise rules.[120] The EU does have a long history of medical device soft law.[121] In the EU, the guidance on the implementation of the MDR defines the line between non-medical device and medical device software.

66. The GDPR has the EDPB,[122] the AIA the European Artificial Intelligence Board[123] and the MDR established the MDCG.[124] See box 3 for an elaboration on the entities regarding the AIA. The MDR bestows the MDCG i.a. with the task of contributing to the development of guidance in view of implementation of the MDR, including the development of guidelines and providing advice in assessment of MDR implementation.[125]

---

118 AIA Annex I (11).

119 Fraser and others (n 22) 483–484.

120 Elisabetta Biasin and Erik Kamenjašević, 'Regulatory Approaches Towards AI-Based Medical Device Cybersecurity: A Transatlantic Perspective' (2024) 15 European Journal of Risk Regulation 881.

121 Ibid 880.

122 GDPR art 68.

123 AIA art 65.

124 MDR art 103(1).

125 MDR art 105(c, e and g).

Box 3 – AI Office, AI Board, advisory forum and scientific panel

The AI Act defines multiple bodies regarding its implementation. The **AI Office** (hereafter: Office) is a function of the Commission.[126] The **European Artificial Intelligence Board** (hereafter: Board) is composed out of representatives of each Member State, as well as the EDPB (though the latter without voting right).[127]

The Office attends meetings of the Board.[128] The Board advises the Commission and Member States on the application of the AIA, i.a. by providing 'recommendations and written opinions on any relevant matters related to the implementation', amongst which 'the development and application of codes of conduct and codes of practice'.[129]

The Commission and Board are further advised by the **advisory forum**, of which the members are appointed by the Commission.[130] Analogously, the Commission has also established the **scientific panel of independent experts**, which will advise the AI Office regarding GPAI models, by i.a. 'alerting the AI Office of possible systemic risks at Union level', and 'contributing to the development of tools and methodologies for evaluating capabilities of [GPAI] models and systems'.[131] The Commission has already adopted rules regarding the set-up of the panel.[132]

67. The MDCG provides clarification for the interpretation of the notion of MDSW in its guidance. It specifies that whether software is used within a healthcare setting is not a decisive condition for it to be MDSW.[133] Instead, software can be classified as MDSW when it is (1) 'intended to process, analyse,

126 AIA art 64(1).
127 AIA art 65(2).
128 AIA art 65(2).
129 AIA art 66(e)(i).
130 AIA art 67(1,3 and 8).
131 AIA art 68(1) and (3)(a).
132 Commission Implementing Regulation (EU) 2025/454 of 7 March 2025 laying down the rules for the application of Regulation (EU) 2024/1689 of the European Parliament and of the Council as regards the establishment of a scientific panel of independent experts in the field of artificial intelligence (2025).
133 Medical Device Coordination Group, *MDCG 2019-11 Guidance on Qualification and Classification of Software in Regulation (EU) 2017/745 – MDR and Regulation (EU) 2017/746 – IVDR* (2019) 6.

create or modify medical information' and (2) 'if the creation or modification of that information is governed by a medical intended purpose'.[134]

68. Caselaw has concretised the intended purpose requirement for medical devices in EU law. Concretely the Court of Justice of the European Union (hereafter: CJEU), ruled that an intended use of measuring physiological variables only suffices the condition of being 'governed by a medical purpose', if the manufacturer intended such measurements to be made for a medical purpose.[135,136] Although the judgment forms part of EU medical-device law, it interprets the Medical Device Directive (hereafter: MDD).[137] The MDR has repealed the MDD, and by contrast with EU data-protection law, the CJEU has not yet confirmed that MDD precedent continues to have binding force under the MDR.[138,139] See box 4 for the difference between European directives and regulations.

69. The use-case entails software that analyses patient comorbidity information, in search of support for an optimal proposal for therapy. Accordingly, the use-case qualifies as software that analyses medical information, governed by a medical intended purpose. Therefore, it constitutes MDSW.

---

134 Ibid 6.

135 Case C-219/11 *Brain Products GmbH v BioSemi VOF and Others* [2012] ECLI:EU:C:2012:742 [33].

136 The CJEU further clarified the 'intended purpose' requirement in *SNITEM and Philips* by holding that medical software (MDSW) need not 'act directly in or on the human body' to qualify as a medical device under the Directive. Case C-329/16 *Syndicat national de l'industrie des technologies médicales (SNITEM) and Philips France v Premier Ministre and Ministre des Affairs sociales et de la Santé* [2017] ECLI:EU:C:2017:947 [40].

137 Council Directive 93/42/EEC of 14 June 1993 concerning medical devices (1993).

138 The MDR became applicable 26 May 2021, subject to transitional arrangements for certain legacy devices until 31 December 2028. MDR art 120 as amended by Regulation (EU) 2023/607 of the European Parliament and of the Council of 15 March 2023 amending Regulations (EU) 2017/745 and (EU) 2017/746 as regards the transitional provisions for certain medical devices and in vitro diagnostic medical devices (2023) art 1.

139 As of this writing (20 June 2025), the CJEU has not yet rendered final judgments interpreting substantive MDR provisions. However, the CJEU cites its DPD-era caselaw in judgments interpreting the GDPR. Chapter 5.1 expands on this. However, some nuance might be in order, as the CJEU recognises that there are 'identical concepts' in both the MDD and MDR. C-589/23 *Cassella-med GmbH & Co. KG, MCM Klosterfrau Vertriebsgesellschaft mbH v Verband Sozialer Wettbewerb eV* [2025] ECLI:EU:C:2025:173 [41–44]. Additionally, the CJEU is expected to render a judgement on a referred question on the scope of the notion of 'medical devices within the meaning of Article 2(1) of [the MDR]'. C/2024/5402 *Request for a preliminary ruling from the Landgericht Bochum (Germany) lodged on 18 June 2024 – Zentrale zur Bekämpfung unlauteren Wettbewerbs Frankfurt am Main eV v Diagramm Halbach GmbH & Co. KG* [2024].

Box 4 – European directives v regulations

The EU creates different types of legal acts. Two of those types are directives and regulations. Whereas a directive requires the Member States of the EU to 'transpose' the 'policy objectives set out in the directive' into the national laws of the Member States themselves, leaving more interpretation to the Member States regarding the implementation; a regulation is 'binding in its entirety and directly applicable'.[140]

Multiple times in its history, the EU created a directive that was later repealed by a similar regulation. These acts of harmonisation include e.g. the MDR (Medical Device Regulation) repealing the MDD (Medical Device Directive) and the GDPR (General Data Protection Regulation) repealing the DPD (Data Protection Directive).

Would a third-party conformity assessment be required according to the MDR?

70. The MDR defines four classes of medical devices: I, IIa, IIb and III; classification of which should be carried out in accordance with Annex VIII.[141] Rule 11 of Annex VIII dictates that software should be classified based on what it is 'intended to' do, as is defined in Table 1.[142]

Table 1. MDSW classification

Intend		Class
'provide information which is used to take decisions with diagnosis or therapeutic purposes'	'if such decisions have impact that may cause: death or an irreversible deterioration of a person's state of health'	III
	'if such decisions have impact that may cause: [...] a serious deterioration of a person's state of health or a surgical intervention'	IIb
	where the software is not Clas III of Class IIb	IIa
'monitor physiological processes'	where such processes are 'vital physiological processes, where the nature of variations of those parameters is such that it could result in immediate danger to the patient'	IIb
	where the software is not Class IIb	IIa
other		I

140 Catherine Barnard and Steve Peers, *European Union Law* (third edn, Oxford University Press 2020) 103–105.

141 MDR art 51(1).

142 MDR Annex VIII (6.3).

71. The use-case does not constitute monitoring software. Hence, the respective classification does not apply. The use-case would constitute software that is intended to provide information which would be used to make a triage decision, which is a decision 'with diagnosis or therapeutic purpose'. Hence it would constitute class II or class III software.

72. As Lengerich et al. explain, a triage decision in the context of the use-case has an impact on mortality.[143] Hence, the decision for which the information provided by the software is used, has impact that may cause death. Hence, the use-case constitutes software of class III.

73. The MDR specifies that class III MDSW 'shall be subject to a conformity assessment as specified in Annex IX' or alternatively 'as specified in Annex X coupled with a conformity assessment as specified in Annex XI'.[144] This work further analyses these procedures in chapter 5.2. The procedures described in annexes IX, X and XI all involve a notified body, which is an independent third party.[145] Therefore, the MDR would require a third-party conformity assessment to precede the use-case. Hence, the AIA would define the use-case to entail an HRAIS.[146]

74. It is easy to overlook that the lack of such a conformity assessment requirement does not guarantee the use-case is *not* a HRAIS.[147] Systems mentioned in Annex III can also be considered HRAISs.[148] Included in those systems are i.a. certain 'patient triage systems'.[149,150] See box 5 and box 6 for the text of Annexes I and III.

Box 5 – AI Annex I – List of Union harmonisation legislation

Section A. List of Union harmonisation legislation based on the New Legislative Framework

1. Directive 2006/42/EC of the European Parliament and of the Council of 17 May 2006 on machinery, and amending Directive 95/16/EC (OJ L 157, 9.6.2006, p. 24);

---

143 Lengerich and others (n 12).
144 MDR art 52(3).
145 MDR Annex IX (2), Annex X (1), Annex XI (6.1 and 14).
146 AIA art 6(1).
147 Sofia Palmieri, 'The Renewed EU Legal Framework for Medical AI' (2024) 15 European Journal of Law and Technology 12.
148 AIA art 6(2).
149 AIA Annex III (5)(d).
150 The AIA defines some derogations when systems do not pose significant harm *and* meet additional conditions as specified in AIA art 6(3).

2. Directive 2009/48/EC of the European Parliament and of the Council of 18 June 2009 on the safety of toys (OJ L 170, 30.6.2009, p. 1);
3. Directive 2013/53/EU of the European Parliament and of the Council of 20 November 2013 on recreational craft and personal watercraft and repealing Directive 94/25/EC (OJ L 354, 28.12.2013, p. 90);
4. Directive 2014/33/EU of the European Parliament and of the Council of 26 February 2014 on the harmonisation of the laws of the Member States relating to lifts and safety components for lifts (OJ L 96, 29.3.2014, p. 251);
5. Directive 2014/34/EU of the European Parliament and of the Council of 26 February 2014 on the harmonisation of the laws of the Member States relating to equipment and protective systems intended for use in potentially explosive atmospheres (OJ L 96, 29.3.2014, p. 309);
6. Directive 2014/53/EU of the European Parliament and of the Council of 16 April 2014 on the harmonisation of the laws of the Member States relating to the making available on the market of radio equipment and repealing Directive 1999/5/EC (OJ L 153, 22.5.2014, p. 62);
7. Directive 2014/68/EU of the European Parliament and of the Council of 15 May 2014 on the harmonisation of the laws of the Member States relating to the making available on the market of pressure equipment (OJ L 189, 27.6.2014, p. 164);
8. Regulation (EU) 2016/424 of the European Parliament and of the Council of 9 March 2016 on cableway installations and repealing Directive 2000/9/EC (OJ L 81, 31.3.2016, p. 1);
9. Regulation (EU) 2016/425 of the European Parliament and of the Council of 9 March 2016 on personal protective equipment and repealing Council Directive 89/686/EEC (OJ L 81, 31.3.2016, p. 51);
10. Regulation (EU) 2016/426 of the European Parliament and of the Council of 9 March 2016 on appliances burning gaseous fuels and repealing Directive 2009/142/EC (OJ L 81, 31.3.2016, p. 99);
11. Regulation (EU) 2017/745 of the European Parliament and of the Council of 5 April 2017 on medical devices, amending Directive 2001/83/EC, Regulation (EC) No 178/2002 and Regulation (EC) No 1223/2009 and repealing Council Directives 90/385/EEC and 93/42/EEC (OJ L 117, 5.5.2017, p. 1);
12. Regulation (EU) 2017/746 of the European Parliament and of the Council of 5 April 2017 on in vitro diagnostic medical devices and repealing Directive 98/79/EC and Commission Decision 2010/227/EU (OJ L 117, 5.5.2017, p. 176).

Section B. List of other Union harmonisation legislation

13. Regulation (EC) No 300/2008 of the European Parliament and of the Council of 11 March 2008 on common rules in the field of civil aviation security and repealing Regulation (EC) No 2320/2002 (OJ L 97, 9.4.2008, p. 72);
14. Regulation (EU) No 168/2013 of the European Parliament and of the Council of 15 January 2013 on the approval and market surveillance of two- or three-wheel vehicles and quadricycles (OJ L 60, 2.3.2013, p. 52);
15. Regulation (EU) No 167/2013 of the European Parliament and of the Council of 5 February 2013 on the approval and market surveillance of agricultural and forestry vehicles (OJ L 60, 2.3.2013, p. 1);
16. Directive 2014/90/EU of the European Parliament and of the Council of 23 July 2014 on marine equipment and repealing Council Directive 96/98/EC (OJ L 257, 28.8.2014, p. 146);
17. Directive (EU) 2016/797 of the European Parliament and of the Council of 11 May 2016 on the interoperability of the rail system within the European Union (OJ L 138, 26.5.2016, p. 44);
18. Regulation (EU) 2018/858 of the European Parliament and of the Council of 30 May 2018 on the approval and market surveillance of motor vehicles and their trailers, and of systems, components and separate technical units intended for such vehicles, amending Regulations (EC) No 715/2007 and (EC) No 595/2009 and repealing Directive 2007/46/EC (OJ L 151, 14.6.2018, p. 1);
19. Regulation (EU) 2019/2144 of the European Parliament and of the Council of 27 November 2019 on type-approval requirements for motor vehicles and their trailers, and systems, components and separate technical units intended for such vehicles, as regards their general safety and the protection of vehicle occupants and vulnerable road users, amending Regulation (EU) 2018/858 of the European Parliament and of the Council and repealing Regulations (EC) No 78/2009, (EC) No 79/2009 and (EC) No 661/2009 of the European Parliament and of the Council and Commission Regulations (EC) No 631/2009, (EU) No 406/2010, (EU) No 672/2010, (EU) No 1003/2010, (EU) No 1005/2010, (EU) No 1008/2010, (EU) No 1009/2010, (EU) No 19/2011, (EU) No 109/2011, (EU) No 458/2011, (EU) No 65/2012, (EU) No 130/2012, (EU) No 347/2012, (EU) No 351/2012, (EU) No 1230/2012 and (EU) 2015/166 (OJ L 325, 16.12.2019, p. 1);

20. Regulation (EU) 2018/1139 of the European Parliament and of the Council of 4 July 2018 on common rules in the field of civil aviation and establishing a European Union Aviation Safety Agency, and amending Regulations (EC) No 2111/2005, (EC) No 1008/2008, (EU) No 996/2010, (EU) No 376/2014 and Directives 2014/30/EU and 2014/53/EU of the European Parliament and of the Council, and repealing Regulations (EC) No 552/2004 and (EC) No 216/2008 of the European Parliament and of the Council and Council Regulation (EEC) No 3922/91 (OJ L 212, 22.8.2018, p. 1), in so far as the design, production and placing on the market of aircrafts referred to in Article 2(1), points (a) and (b) thereof, where it concerns unmanned aircraft and their engines, propellers, parts and equipment to control them remotely, are concerned.

Box 6 – AI Annex III – High-risk AI systems referred to in Article 6(2)

High-risk AI systems pursuant to Article 6(2) are the AI systems listed in any of the following areas:

1. Biometrics, in so far as their use is permitted under relevant Union or national law:
   (a) remote biometric identification systems.

   This shall not include AI systems intended to be used for biometric verification the sole purpose of which is to confirm that a specific natural person is the person he or she claims to be;

   (b) AI systems intended to be used for biometric categorisation, according to sensitive or protected attributes or characteristics based on the inference of those attributes or characteristics;
   (c) AI systems intended to be used for emotion recognition.
2. Critical infrastructure: AI systems intended to be used as safety components in the management and operation of critical digital infrastructure, road traffic, or in the supply of water, gas, heating or electricity.
3. Education and vocational training:
   (a) AI systems intended to be used to determine access or admission or to assign natural persons to educational and vocational training institutions at all levels;
   (b) AI systems intended to be used to evaluate learning outcomes, including when those outcomes are used to steer the learning process of natural persons in educational and vocational training institutions at all levels;

(c) AI systems intended to be used for the purpose of assessing the appropriate level of education that an individual will receive or will be able to access, in the context of or within educational and vocational training institutions at all levels;
(d) AI systems intended to be used for monitoring and detecting prohibited behaviour of students during tests in the context of or within educational and vocational training institutions at all levels.

4. Employment, workers' management and access to self-employment:
(a) AI systems intended to be used for the recruitment or selection of natural persons, in particular to place targeted job advertisements, to analyse and filter job applications, and to evaluate candidates;
(b) AI systems intended to be used to make decisions affecting terms of work-related relationships, the promotion or termination of work-related contractual relationships, to allocate tasks based on individual behaviour or personal traits or characteristics or to monitor and evaluate the performance and behaviour of persons in such relationships.

5. Access to and enjoyment of essential private services and essential public services and benefits:
(a) AI systems intended to be used by public authorities or on behalf of public authorities to evaluate the eligibility of natural persons for essential public assistance benefits and services, including healthcare services, as well as to grant, reduce, revoke, or reclaim such benefits and services;
(b) AI systems intended to be used to evaluate the creditworthiness of natural persons or establish their credit score, with the exception of AI systems used for the purpose of detecting financial fraud;
(c) AI systems intended to be used for risk assessment and pricing in relation to natural persons in the case of life and health insurance;
(d) AI systems intended to evaluate and classify emergency calls by natural persons or to be used to dispatch, or to establish priority in the dispatching of, emergency first response services, including by police, firefighters and medical aid, as well as of emergency healthcare patient triage systems.

6. Law enforcement, in so far as their use is permitted under relevant Union or national law:
(a) AI systems intended to be used by or on behalf of law enforcement authorities, or by Union institutions, bodies, offices or agencies in support of law enforcement authorities or on their behalf to assess the risk of a natural person becoming the victim of criminal offences;

(b) AI systems intended to be used by or on behalf of law enforcement authorities or by Union institutions, bodies, offices or agencies in support of law enforcement authorities as polygraphs or similar tools;
(c) AI systems intended to be used by or on behalf of law enforcement authorities, or by Union institutions, bodies, offices or agencies, in support of law enforcement authorities to evaluate the reliability of evidence in the course of the investigation or prosecution of criminal offences;
(d) AI systems intended to be used by law enforcement authorities or on their behalf or by Union institutions, bodies, offices or agencies in support of law enforcement authorities for assessing the risk of a natural person offending or re-offending not solely on the basis of the profiling of natural persons as referred to in Article 3(4) of Directive (EU) 2016/680, or to assess personality traits and characteristics or past criminal behaviour of natural persons or groups;
(e) AI systems intended to be used by or on behalf of law enforcement authorities or by Union institutions, bodies, offices or agencies in support of law enforcement authorities for the profiling of natural persons as referred to in Article 3(4) of Directive (EU) 2016/680 in the course of the detection, investigation or prosecution of criminal offences.

7. Migration, asylum and border control management, in so far as their use is permitted under relevant Union or national law:
(a) AI systems intended to be used by or on behalf of competent public authorities or by Union institutions, bodies, offices or agencies as polygraphs or similar tools;
(b) AI systems intended to be used by or on behalf of competent public authorities or by Union institutions, bodies, offices or agencies to assess a risk, including a security risk, a risk of irregular migration, or a health risk, posed by a natural person who intends to enter or who has entered into the territory of a Member State;
(c) AI systems intended to be used by or on behalf of competent public authorities or by Union institutions, bodies, offices or agencies to assist competent public authorities for the examination of applications for asylum, visa or residence permits and for associated complaints with regard to the eligibility of the natural persons applying for a status, including related assessments of the reliability of evidence;
(d) AI systems intended to be used by or on behalf of competent public authorities, or by Union institutions, bodies, offices or agencies, in the context of migration, asylum or border control management,

for the purpose of detecting, recognising or identifying natural persons, with the exception of the verification of travel documents.

8. Administration of justice and democratic processes:
   (a) AI systems intended to be used by a judicial authority or on their behalf to assist a judicial authority in researching and interpreting facts and the law and in applying the law to a concrete set of facts, or to be used in a similar way in alternative dispute resolution;
   (b) AI systems intended to be used for influencing the outcome of an election or referendum or the voting behaviour of natural persons in the exercise of their vote in elections or referenda. This does not include AI systems to the output of which natural persons are not directly exposed, such as tools used to organise, optimize or structure political campaigns from an administrative or logistical point of view.

4.3.1.B. Requirements Arising from the AI Act

75. The AIA requires providers of HRAISs to ensure that their HRAISs are compliant with the requirements set out in section 2; section 2 being art 8–15.[151] AIA art 8(1) specifies this as: '[HRAISs] shall comply with the requirements laid down in this Section, taking into account their intended purpose as well as the generally acknowledged state of the art on AI and AI-related technologies'.

76. The requirements are then further defined in the rest of section 2 and relate to multiple facets.[152] One of those is the set of requirements on '[a]ccuracy, robustness and cybersecurity', described in art 15. In those requirements, the aspect of *traditional accuracy* is reflected in art 15(1):

> '[HRAISs] shall be designed and developed in such a way that they achieve an appropriate level of accuracy, robustness, and cybersecurity, and that they perform consistently in those respects throughout their lifecycle.'

77. The aspect of *feedback* is an important requirement e.g. for predictive policing systems.[153,154] It is an effect of output on input during deployment of the system. Therefore, *feedback* accuracy involves aspects of the system's

151 AIA art 16(a).
152 AIA art 9–15 set forth requirements on i.a. the risk management system, data and data governance, technical documentation, record-keeping, transparency, provision of information to deployers and human oversight.
153 Ensign and others (n 5).
154 Hung and Yen (n 52).

lifecycle after placement on the market. The condition in art 15(1) on consistent performance throughout the system's lifecycle could therefore be supportive of *feedback* accuracy, but is however not sufficient as it does not explicitly require taking into account other aspects than *input accuracy*. Be that as it may, art 15(4) refers to *feedback*, hence the AIA covers it through that provision. See box 7 for the full text of art 15.

Box 7 – AI Act art 15 – Accuracy, robustness and cybersecurity

1. **High-risk AI systems shall be designed and developed in such a way that they achieve an appropriate level of accuracy, robustness, and cybersecurity**, and that they perform **consistently** in those respects **throughout their lifecycle.**
2. To address the technical aspects of how to measure the appropriate levels of accuracy and robustness set out in paragraph 1 and any other relevant performance metrics, the Commission shall, in cooperation with relevant stakeholders and organisations such as metrology and benchmarking authorities, encourage, as appropriate, the development of benchmarks and measurement methodologies.
3. **The levels of accuracy and the relevant accuracy metrics of high-risk AI systems shall be declared in the accompanying instructions of use.**
4. **High-risk AI systems shall be as resilient** as possible **regarding errors, faults or inconsistencies that may occur within the system or the environment in which the system operates, in particular due to their interaction with natural persons or other systems. Technical and organisational measures shall be taken in this regard.**

   The robustness of high-risk AI systems may be achieved through technical redundancy solutions, which may include backup or fail-safe plans.

   High-risk AI systems that continue to learn after being placed on the market or put into service shall be developed in such a way as to eliminate or reduce as far as possible the risk of possibly **biased outputs influencing input for future operations (feedback loops)**, and as to ensure that any such feedback loops are duly addressed with appropriate mitigation measures.
5. High-risk AI systems shall be resilient against attempts by unauthorised third parties to alter their use, outputs or performance by exploiting system vulnerabilities.

   The technical solutions aiming to ensure the cybersecurity of high-risk AI systems shall be appropriate to the relevant circumstances and the risks.

The technical solutions to address AI specific vulnerabilities shall include, where appropriate, measures to prevent, detect, respond to, resolve and control for attacks trying to manipulate the training data set (data poisoning), or pre-trained components used in training (model poisoning), inputs designed to cause the AI model to make a mistake (adversarial examples or model evasion), confidentiality attacks or model flaws.

Box 8 – AI Act art 10 – Data and data governance

1. **High-risk AI systems** which make use of techniques involving the training of AI models with data **shall be developed on the basis of training, validation and testing data sets that meet the quality criteria referred to in paragraphs 2 to 5** whenever such data sets are used.
2. **Training, validation and testing data sets shall be subject to data governance and management practices appropriate for the intended purpose** of the high-risk AI system. **Those practices shall concern** in particular:
   (a) **the relevant design choices**;
   (b) data collection processes and the origin of data, and in the case of personal data, the original purpose of the data collection;
   (c) **relevant data-preparation processing operations**, such as **annotation, labelling, cleaning, updating, enrichment and aggregation**;
   (d) the **formulation of assumptions**, in particular **with respect to the information that the data are supposed to measure and represent**;
   (e) an assessment of the **availability, quantity and suitability** of the **data sets that are needed**;
   (f) **examination** in view of possible **biases** that are **likely to affect the health and safety** of persons, **have a negative impact on fundamental rights or** lead to **discrimination** prohibited under Union law, **especially where data outputs influence inputs for future operations**;
   (g) appropriate **measures to detect, prevent and mitigate** possible **biases identified according to point (f)**;
   (h) the **identification of relevant data gaps or shortcomings** that prevent compliance with this Regulation, **and how those** gaps and **shortcomings can be addressed**.
3. **Training, validation and testing data sets shall be relevant, sufficiently representative**, and to the best extent possible, **free of errors and complete in view of the intended purpose**. They shall have the

appropriate statistical properties, including, where applicable, as regards the persons or groups of persons in relation to whom the high-risk AI system is intended to be used. Those characteristics of the data sets may be met at the level of individual data sets or at the level of a combination thereof.

4. **Data sets shall take into account, to the extent required by the intended purpose, the characteristics or elements that are particular to the specific geographical, contextual, behavioural or functional setting within which the high-risk AI system is intended to be used.**
5. To the extent that it is strictly necessary for the purpose of ensuring bias detection and correction in relation to the high-risk AI systems in accordance with paragraph (2), points (f) and (g) of this Article, the providers of such systems may exceptionally process special categories of personal data, subject to appropriate safeguards for the fundamental rights and freedoms of natural persons. In addition to the provisions set out in Regulations (EU) 2016/679 and (EU) 2018/1725 and Directive (EU) 2016/680, all the following conditions must be met in order for such processing to occur:
   (a) the bias detection and correction cannot be effectively fulfilled by processing other data, including synthetic or anonymised data;
   (b) the special categories of personal data are subject to technical limitations on the re-use of the personal data, and state-of-the-art security and privacy-preserving measures, including pseudonymisation;
   (c) the special categories of personal data are subject to measures to ensure that the personal data processed are secured, protected, subject to suitable safeguards, including strict controls and documentation of the access, to avoid misuse and ensure that only authorised persons have access to those personal data with appropriate confidentiality obligations;
   (d) the special categories of personal data are not to be transmitted, transferred or otherwise accessed by other parties;
   (e) the special categories of personal data are deleted once the bias has been corrected or the personal data has reached the end of its retention period, whichever comes first;
   (f) the records of processing activities pursuant to Regulations (EU) 2016/679 and (EU) 2018/1725 and Directive (EU) 2016/680 include the reasons why the processing of special categories of personal data was strictly necessary to detect and correct biases, and why that objective could not be achieved by processing other data.
6. For the development of high-risk AI systems not using techniques involving the training of AI models, paragraphs 2 to 5 apply only to the testing data sets.

78. Also art 10 addresses accuracy. See box 8 for the full text of art 10. Art 10(2)(c) on data-preparation addresses *input accuracy* by requiring appropriate data processing 'such as annotation, labelling, cleaning, updating, enrichment and aggregation'. This can be illustrated with the example in chapter 3 on fish species. Should the data have been properly cleaned (i.a. background removal), the inaccuracy might have been reduced *in casu*.

79. Art 10(3) as well, points to a requirement on data being close to reality, stating that '[t]raining, validation and testing data sets shall be relevant, sufficiently representative, and to the best extent possible, free of errors and complete'. Because training and testing data have both an input and an output aspect, that requirement relates both to *input accuracy* and *traditional accuracy*.

80. Additionally, art 10(2)(a) adds a requirement on relevant design choices. However, the design choices do not refer to design choices regarding the AI system itself, rather the data governance and management practices which the used data sets are subject to. This work analyses whether this might point implicitly to *feedback* or *proxy choice* in how it is further defined by the AIA. That concretisation is given in harmonised standards, which the following chapter describes.

81. Beyond section 2, the AIA sets forth additional requirements for providers of HRAISs, not all of which address accuracy.[155] Some of those requirements do have an indirect link with accuracy, e.g.: art 16(f) requires the provider to ensure that the HRAIS undergoes the relevant conformity assessment procedure as referred to in art 43.

82. Art 43 describes the options providers of HRAISs have regarding demonstration of conformity with the requirements in section 2. The article divides HRAISs into four types. Annex I of this book provides an analysis of the options regarding conformity assessment that art 43 sets forth for each of those types. The use-case entails an HRAIS listed in section A of AIA Annex I. Art 43 would require the provider in the use-case to (i) 'follow the relevant conformity assessment procedure as required under [the MDR]', (ii) abide by and include in that procedure '[t]he requirements set out in Section 2' and (iii) perform '[p]oints 4.4., 4.5. and the fifth paragraph of point 4.6' of the conformity assessment procedure described in Annex VII. Therefore, the provider in the use-case would be required, other than is already required by the MDR, to (a) abide by the requirements described in art 8-15, as well as include assessment of those requirements in the conformity assessment procedure pursuant to

[155] AIA art 16(b, d, e, g, l) and art 22 require providers of HRAISs to indicate information regarding the origin of the AI system, keep documentation and logs, draw up an EU declaration of conformity, comply with registration obligations, ensure compliance with requirements regarding accessibility and follow certain rules on authorised representatives.

the MDR, and (b) perform the aforementioned points of assessment described in AIA Annex VII. Those points set forth requirements on assessment of the technical documentation.[156] Other than a procedural aspect regarding *input accuracy* in the fifth paragraph of point 4.6, this assessment adds no explicit accuracy requirements.[157] The other requirements for providers set forth by the AIA outside of section 2 similarly concern procedural aspects of accuracy, rather than addressing aspects that have not been covered in section 2.[158]

83. The obligations described above apply to providers of HRAISs. The AIA also sets forth requirements for deployers of HRAISs.[159] The hospital using the triage tool in the use-case would be subject to these obligations. Art 26(4), in particular, addresses *input accuracy*, stipulating that 'to the extent the deployer exercises control over the input data, that deployer shall ensure that input data is relevant and sufficiently representative in view of the intended purpose'. See box 9 for the text of AIA art 26.

84. In conclusion, the AIA itself has notions of accuracy regarding HRAISs that differ between the one regarding providers and the one regarding deployers. Providers need to account for *traditional accuracy*, *input accuracy* and *feedback*. Deployers, to a more limited extent, need to account for *input accuracy*. *Subgoal robustness* is not directly mentioned with regard to HRAISs and whether a requirement regarding *proxy choice* is present is not explicitly clear. However, the analysis finds that the AIA refers to harmonised standards for the further interpretation of these requirements, which the next part elaborates upon.

---

156 AIA Annex VII [4].

157 AIA Annex VII [4.6], fifth para requires '[w]here the AI system does not meet the requirement relating to the data used to train it, re-training [...] prior to the application for a new conformity assessment' and explanation of the notified body regarding 'considerations on the [data quality] used'.

158 Art 16(c) requires providers to have a quality management system in place which complies with art 17; art 17(1)(g) requires the system to include a risk management system as defined in art 9, which is part of section 2, as well as a post-market monitoring system as described in art 73; art 73(2) requires that system to 'evaluate the continuous compliance of AI systems with the requirements set out in [...] Section 2'; and art 16(j) finally requires the provider only to take certain actions when he 'ha[s] reason to consider that [the HRAIS] is not in conformity with [the AIA]' (art 20(1)) or 'becomes aware of' certain risks (art 20(2)).

159 AIA art 26 requires deployers of HRAISs to take appropriate technical and organisation measures; assign (appropriate) human oversight; insure that input data is relevant and sufficiently representative; monitor the operation; inform certain actors in certain situations, suspend the use in certain situations; keep logs; provide information in less than 48 hours in certain situations; inform natural persons that are subject to the use; and cooperate with competent authorities.

Box 9 – AI Act art 26 – Obligations of deployers of high-risk AI systems

1. **Deployers of high-risk AI systems shall take appropriate technical and organisational measures to ensure they use such systems in accordance with the instructions for use** accompanying the systems, pursuant to paragraphs 3 and 6.
2. Deployers shall assign human oversight to natural persons who have the necessary competence, training and authority, as well as the necessary support.
3. The obligations set out in paragraphs 1 and 2, are without prejudice to other deployer obligations under Union or national law and to the deployer's freedom to organise its own resources and activities for the purpose of implementing the human oversight measures indicated by the provider.
4. Without prejudice to paragraphs 1 and 2, **to the extent the deployer exercises control over the input data, that deployer shall ensure that input data is relevant and sufficiently representative in view of the intended purpose of the high-risk AI system.**
5. Deployers shall monitor the operation of the high-risk AI system on the basis of the instructions for use and, where relevant, inform providers in accordance with Article 72. Where deployers have reason to consider that the use of the high-risk AI system in accordance with the instructions may result in that AI system presenting a risk within the meaning of Article 79(1), they shall, without undue delay, inform the provider or distributor and the relevant market surveillance authority, and shall suspend the use of that system. Where deployers have identified a serious incident, they shall also immediately inform first the provider, and then the importer or distributor and the relevant market surveillance authorities of that incident. If the deployer is not able to reach the provider, Article 73 shall apply mutatis mutandis. This obligation shall not cover sensitive operational data of deployers of AI systems which are law enforcement authorities.

   For deployers that are financial institutions subject to requirements regarding their internal governance, arrangements or processes under Union financial services law, the monitoring obligation set out in the first subparagraph shall be deemed to be fulfilled by complying with the rules on internal governance arrangements, processes and mechanisms pursuant to the relevant financial service law.
6. Deployers of high-risk AI systems shall keep the logs automatically generated by that high-risk AI system to the extent such logs are under their control, for a period appropriate to the intended purpose of the high-risk AI system, of at least six months, unless provided otherwise in applicable Union or national law, in particular in Union law on the protection of personal data.

Deployers that are financial institutions subject to requirements regarding their internal governance, arrangements or processes under Union financial services law shall maintain the logs as part of the documentation kept pursuant to the relevant Union financial service law.

7. Before putting into service or using a high-risk AI system at the workplace, deployers who are employers shall inform workers' representatives and the affected workers that they will be subject to the use of the high-risk AI system. This information shall be provided, where applicable, in accordance with the rules and procedures laid down in Union and national law and practice on information of workers and their representatives.
8. Deployers of high-risk AI systems that are public authorities, or Union institutions, bodies, offices or agencies shall comply with the registration obligations referred to in Article 49. When such deployers find that the high-risk AI system that they envisage using has not been registered in the EU database referred to in Article 71, they shall not use that system and shall inform the provider or the distributor.
9. Where applicable, deployers of high-risk AI systems shall use the information provided under Article 13 of this Regulation to comply with their obligation to carry out a data protection impact assessment under Article 35 of Regulation (EU) 2016/679 or Article 27 of Directive (EU) 2016/680.
10. Without prejudice to Directive (EU) 2016/680, in the framework of an investigation for the targeted search of a person suspected or convicted of having committed a criminal offence, the deployer of a high-risk AI system for post-remote biometric identification shall request an authorisation, *ex ante*, or without undue delay and no later than 48 hours, by a judicial authority or an administrative authority whose decision is binding and subject to judicial review, for the use of that system, except when it is used for the initial identification of a potential suspect based on objective and verifiable facts directly linked to the offence. Each use shall be limited to what is strictly necessary for the investigation of a specific criminal offence.

    If the authorisation requested pursuant to the first subparagraph is rejected, the use of the post-remote biometric identification system linked to that requested authorisation shall be stopped with immediate effect and the personal data linked to the use of the high-risk AI system for which the authorisation was requested shall be deleted.

    In no case shall such high-risk AI system for post-remote biometric identification be used for law enforcement purposes in an untargeted way, without any link to a criminal offence, a criminal proceeding, a genuine and present or genuine and foreseeable threat of a criminal offence, or the search for a specific missing person. It shall be ensured that no decision that produces an adverse legal effect on a person may be taken by the law enforcement authorities based solely on the output of such post-remote biometric identification systems.

This paragraph is without prejudice to Article 9 of Regulation (EU) 2016/679 and Article 10 of Directive (EU) 2016/680 for the processing of biometric data.

Regardless of the purpose or deployer, each use of such high-risk AI systems shall be documented in the relevant police file and shall be made available to the relevant market surveillance authority and the national data protection authority upon request, excluding the disclosure of sensitive operational data related to law enforcement. This subparagraph shall be without prejudice to the powers conferred by Directive (EU) 2016/680 on supervisory authorities.

Deployers shall submit annual reports to the relevant market surveillance and national data protection authorities on their use of post-remote biometric identification systems, excluding the disclosure of sensitive operational data related to law enforcement. The reports may be aggregated to cover more than one deployment.

Member States may introduce, in accordance with Union law, more restrictive laws on the use of post-remote biometric identification systems.

11. Without prejudice to Article 50 of this Regulation, deployers of high-risk AI systems referred to in Annex III that make decisions or assist in making decisions related to natural persons shall inform the natural persons that they are subject to the use of the high-risk AI system. For high-risk AI systems used for law enforcement purposes Article 13 of Directive (EU) 2016/680 shall apply.
12. Deployers shall cooperate with the relevant competent authorities in any action those authorities take in relation to the high-risk AI system in order to implement this Regulation.

4.3.1.C. Beyond the Regulation: The State of the Art and Harmonised Standards

85. The AIA refers to harmonised standards in two ways: through a presumption of conformity and in referring to the SoTA. The following two parts address each respectively.

Harmonised standards in the presumption of conformity

86. The above-mentioned requirements are situated in section 2 of the AIA.[160] Art 40 stipulates that HRAISs 'shall be presumed to be in conformity with the requirements set out in Section 2' if they 'are in conformity with harmonised standards or parts thereof the references of which have been published in the Official Journal of the European Union [hereafter: OJEU] in accordance with Regulation (EU) No 1025/2012'.[161]

87. EU Regulation 1025/2012 (hereafter: the Standardisation Regulation), establishes rules on European standardisation.[162] The Standardisation Regulation defines harmonised standards as follows:[163]

> 'technical specification[s,] adopted by a [European standardisation organisation], for repeated or continuous application, with which compliance is not compulsory[,] on the basis of a request made by the Commission for the application of Union harmonisation legislation.'

88. The standardisation organisations are defined in rec 4: 'European standards are adopted by the European standardisation organisations, namely CEN, Cenelec and ETSI'. The Commission has made a standardisation request as referred to in art 2(1) of the Standardisation Regulation.[164] In the standardisation request, the list of deliverables includes: 'European standard(s) and/or European standardisation deliverable(s) on accuracy specifications for AI systems'.[165] The Commission requests the European Committee for Standardisation (hereafter: CEN) and the European Committee for Electrotechnical Standardisation (hereafter: CENELEC) to draft the new standards, further specifying the requirements therefore in Annex II of the request.[166] Annex II specifies the requirements regarding accuracy as follows:[167]

---

160 Except for *input accuracy* requirements for deployers (AIA art 26(4)).

161 AIA art 40(1).

162 Regulation (EU) No 1025/2012 of the European Parliament and of the Council of 25 October 2012 on European standardisation, amending Council Directives 89/686/EEC and 93/15/EEC and Directives 94/9/EC, 94/25/EC, 95/16/EC, 97/23/EC, 98/34/EC, 2004/22/EC, 2007/23/EC, 2009/23/EC and 2009/105/EC of the European Parliament and of the Council and repealing Council Decision 87/95/EEC and Decision No 1673/2006/EC of the European Parliament and of the Council (2012).

163 Standardisation Regulation art 2(1).

164 European Commission, Commission Implementing Decision (EU) of 22.5.2023 on a standardisation request to the European Committee for Standardisation and the European Committee for Electrotechnical Standardisation in support of Union policy on artificial intelligence C(2023)3215 (22 May 2023).

165 Ibid Annex I.

166 Ibid art 1.

167 Ibid Annex II (2.6).

> 'For the purpose of this (these) European standard(s) or European standardisation deliverable(s), "accuracy" shall be understood as referring to the capability of the AI system to perform the task for which it has been designed. This should not be confused with the narrower definition of statistical accuracy, which is one of several possible metrics for evaluating the performance of AI systems.'

89. CEN-CENELEC has accepted the standardisation request and established the CEN-CENELEC Joint Technical Committee 21 'Artificial Intelligence' (hereafter: JTC 21).[168] JTC 21 developed a strategic framework to structure its work into three main building blocks: Foundational Standards, Engineering and Conformity Assessment; where Engineering includes Technical requirements i.a. on accuracy.[169] JTC 21 working group 3 'Engineering aspects' has since developed multiple standards, including *Information technology – Artificial intelligence (AI) – Bias in AI systems and AI aided decision making* (ISO/IEC TR 24027:2021).[170] It is also working on other standards, i.a. ISO/IEC 23282 *Artificial Intelligence – Evaluation methods for accurate natural language processing systems.*[171] However, at the time of writing, those are not yet published in the OJEU and hence do not yet provide a basis for a presumption of conformity.[172]

90. The Joint Research Centre of the Commission (hereafter: JRC) notes that coverage of existing ISO/IEC standards on i.a. accuracy is limited.[173] The JRC Technical Report does add however that i.a. accuracy is in scope of the work items of the JTC 21, referring i.a. to ISO/IEC 23282 *Artificial Intelligence – Evaluation methods for accurate natural language processing systems.*[174] The JRC report also describes the notion of accuracy in the AIA:[175]

> 'Some other terms may be used both in legal documentation with a broader meaning as in technical standards. An example of this would be the term accuracy, which in the AI Act refers to the capability of the AI system to perform the task for which it has been designed, and in ISO/IEC 23053 is given a narrower definition corresponding to

---

168 CEN-CENELEC, 'Artificial Intelligence' <https://www.cencenelec.eu/areas-of-work/cen-cenelec-topics/artificial-intelligence/> accessed 28 January 2025.

169 CEN-CENELEC Joint Technical Committee 21 'Artificial Intelligence', *Business Plan for JTC 21* (16 March 2022) 6–7.

170 CEN-CENELEC Joint Technical Committee 21 Working Group 3, *Information technology – Artificial intelligence (AI) – Bias in AI systems and AI aided decision making (ISO/IEC TR 24027:2021)* (17 December 2023).

171 CEN-CENELEC, 'CEN/CLC/JTC 21/WG 3 Work programme' <https://standards.cencenelec.eu/dyn/www/f?p=205:22:0::::FSP_ORG_ID,FSP_LANG_ID:3125028,25&cs=1DA476872963BA59ED30E0D391D01B7D5> accessed 28 January 2025.

172 AIA art 40(1).

173 European Commission Joint Research Centre, *JRC Technical Report: Analysis of the preliminary AI standardisation work plan in support of the AI Act* (2023) 13.

174 Ibid 14–15.

175 Ibid 24.

statistical accuracy, one of several possible metrics for evaluating the performance of [an] AI system.'

91. As described above, the Commission echoed that interpretation of accuracy in its harmonisation request.[176] Also, in a more recent report in 2024 the JRC notes that both drafting of many of the requested standards as well as an update to the standardisation request would be underway.[177] However, as the aforementioned standards have not yet been finalised and published in the OJEU as of this writing, they currently do not apply yet.

Harmonised standards in the state of the art

92. There is another way through which the AIA refers to harmonised standards. Art 8(1) links the notion of accuracy in section 2 to the SoTA:

> '[HRAISs] shall comply with the requirements laid down in this Section, taking into account their intended purpose as well as the generally acknowledged state of the art on AI and AI-related technologies.'

93. The AIA refers to the SoTA multiple times when defining requirements, but does not define it in its articles, hence this work analyses the recitals for interpretation. Only rec 121 defines the SoTA, which it does as follows:

> 'Compliance with harmonised standards as defined in Article 2, point (1)(c), of [the Standardisation Regulation], which are normally expected to reflect the state of the art, should be a means for providers to demonstrate conformity with the requirements of this Regulation.'

94. Therefore, a source for further interpretation of the notion of accuracy in the AIA regarding HRAIS providers, might be found in harmonised standards. The AIA does not require the standards to be *sui generis* AI standards, but does require that 'the references of [the harmonised standard in question] have been published in the [OJEU] in accordance with [the Standardisation Regulation]'.[178]

95. Multiple harmonised standards have been published in the OJEU based on standardisation requests for other legislation. Considering the lack of AIA *sui generis* published harmonised standards, this work looks further for the

---

176 European Commission, Commission Implementing Decision (EU) of 22.5.2023 on a standardisation request to the European Committee for Standardisation and the European Committee for Electrotechnical Standardisation in support of Union policy on artificial intelligence C(2023)3215 (22 May 2023) Annex II.

177 European Commission Joint Research Centre, *JRC 139430 Harmonised Standards for the European AI Act* (24 October 2024) 2.

178 AIA art 40(1).

specification of the notion of accuracy of the AIA, in harmonised standards relating to accuracy for the MDR. This book provides an analysis of the different implementing decisions that lead to the current MDR harmonised standards in Annex II. The findings show that, as of this writing, 32 such standards are published, which are listed in Annex II of this work.

96. Whilst these harmonised standards do not directly define the notion of accuracy, one of those harmonised standards, No 10, ISO13485,[179] indirectly defines the notion of accuracy as follows. ISO13485 describes i.a. the implementation requirements regarding quality management systems. It states in clause 5.1 that '[t]op management shall provide evidence of its commitment to the development and implementation of the quality management system [i.a.] by establishing the quality policy'. Below, this work describes how the details regarding such quality policy imply aspects of the notion of accuracy.

97. ISO13485 clause 7.2 specifies that the organisation shall determine 'requirements not stated by the customer but necessary for specified or intended use, as known' and 'user training needed to ensure specified performance and safe use of the medical device', as well as ensure such training 'is available or planned to be available'. Thereby ISO13485 takes into account the intended purpose; as well as echoes AIA art 4 on AI literacy needs.

98. Clause 7.2 implies that an organisation needs to foresee requirements even if another party implementing their system does not request it. However, the harmonised standard does not require a specific statistical method to be used. It also does not specify how objectives are to be chosen or measured.

99. Other organisational requirements are also specified, e.g. documentation requirements in clause 4.2. Thereby it is implied that the organisation needs to document how a proxy is chosen and how accuracy of the output is measured against that proxy. As implied by clause 7.2, the provider of the HRAIS cannot, in such documentation, hide behind the inability of a client to request a more appropriate proxy. However, ISO13485 requires the proxy to be appropriate to the documented intended use 'as known'.[180] Therefore, in the use-case, a proxy choice of *mortality given comorbidity* might suffice for the entity offering the use-case on the EU market, if the documented intended use is e.g. prediction of number of deaths in the hospital in order to plan logistical aspects not related to the provision of care of living patients.

100. This is different for the hospital in the use-case. Should it need to abide by this harmonised standard, when implementing the system with the intended

[179] EN ISO 13485:2016/A11:2021, *Medical devices – Quality management systems – Requirements for regulatory purposes* (2021).

[180] ISO13485 clause 7.2 and clause 8.1.

use to *inform triage personnel about the potential beneficial effect of treatment*, it would be required to foresee whether a *mortality given comorbidity* proxy would suffice, *quod non*. However, the hospital in the use-case is the deployer and it is only the provider that needs to abide by AIA art 15 and art 10, taking into account the SoTA.

101. In conclusion, the AIA, via ISO13485, implicitly takes into account *proxy choice*, but not equally for all actors. For example, in the use-case, the provider would be required to properly document the intended use and choose an appropriate proxy for that use. This echoes AIA art 13 on HRAISs being accompanied by instructions for use that include the intended purpose of the system.[181] But the provider would not be required to foresee that the deployer uses the system as intended. See box 10 for a comparison between instructions for use and technical documentation.

Box 10 – Instructions for use v Technical documentation

The AIA defines the **instructions for use** as 'the information provided by the provider to inform the deployer of, in particular, an AI system's intended purpose and proper use'.[182] Whereas **technical documentation** is defined only indirectly; i.a. as one of the sources for specifications of i.a. the intended purpose.[183]

Providers of HRAISs are required accompany their HRAISs with instructions for use.[184] Deployers of HRAISs are required to 'take appropriate technical and organisational measures to ensure they use such systems in accordance with the instructions for use accompanying the system'.[185]

Providers of a HRAIS are also required to draw up technical documentation 'before that system is placed on the market or put into service'.[186] Providers are required to 'keep [the technical documentation] at the disposal of the national competent authorities'.[187] The technical documentation can be assessed by a notified body regarding some HRAISs in light of a conformity assessment.[188] Notified bodies in turn have obligations regarding information actions considering technical documentation towards notifying authorities.[189]

---

181 AIA art 13(3)(b)(i).
182 AIA art 3(15).
183 AIA art 3 (12).
184 AIA art 13(2), art 8(1) and art 16(e).
185 AIA art 26 (1).
186 AIA art 11(1), art 8(1) and art 16(e).
187 AIA art 18(1)(a).
188 AIA art 43 (1), first subpara, point (b) and Annex VII [4.3].
189 AIA art 45(1).

Some particular deployers of HRAISs have additional obligations considering a fundamental rights impact assessment wherein they must have regard for the instructions for use.[190] Additionally, providers of GPAI models are similarly required to draw up technical documentation.[191] Nevertheless, note that these requirements on technical documentation, in contrast to those on instructions for use, do not entail access to the technical documentation by the deployer.

102. On the other hand, AIA art 26(1) stipulates that deployers 'shall take appropriate technical and organisational measures to ensure they use [the HRAIS] in accordance with the instructions for use'. Not included in this obligation regarding deployers are: ensuring the system is accurate in a traditional sense, guarding input data quality the deployer exercises no control over, taking into account feedback loops and checking whether the proxy chosen by the provider is appropriate in the deployer's implementation.[192] Therefore, it is implicitly required that the provider chooses an appropriate proxy and specifies the intended purpose appropriate with the chosen proxy, while the deployer must abide by the instructions including the intended purpose.[193] But it is, at least explicitly, not required that the deployer checks whether the proxy chosen for the intended purpose is appropriate in their implementation.[194] This might lead to unintended consequences, which can be illustrated with the following fictional example:

1. Provider assumes intended purpose is purely aid of logistical operations, not related to caregiving for living patients;
2. **Provider *defines intended purpose as: aid in estimation of probability that a patient will die*;**
3. Provider checks that the system is accurate in a traditional sense;

190 AIA art 27(1)(e).
191 AIA art 53(1)(a).
192 AIA art 13(3)(b)(ii, v and vi) require description of the 'level of accuracy', describing output-proxy distance or *traditional accuracy* the provider claims, and 'performance regarding specific persons or groups of persons on which the system is intended to be used', as well as 'specifications for the input data', relating to the *input accuracy* obligation applicable to deployers.
193 This is further strengthened by the obligation for providers to describe 'the overall expected level of accuracy in relation to its intended purpose' in the technical documentation, an obligation that implicitly requires to describe the chosen proxy, as by AIA Annex IV [3].
194 AIA art 26(1) corroborates this by stipulating that '[d]eployers of [HRAISs] shall take appropriate technical and organisational measures to ensure they use such systems in accordance with the instructions for use', without referring to the technical documentation, in which the chosen proxy might be described, as by Annex IV [3].

4. Provider checks that the input data is of high quality and is i.a. representative of the population it is to be used on;
5. Provider concludes that no feedback issues will arise as the system does not learn once in operation;
6. **Deployer** *in concreto* implements the system as a triage aid system and ***defines intended purpose as: aid in estimation of probability that a patient will die***;
7. Deployer checks that the input data is of high quality and is i.a. representative of the population it is to be used on.

103. The actor who executes step 6 would infringe on the requirements regarding *proxy choice* should it be the provider that follows such reasoning. However, because the deployer is making this reasoning, no explicit requirement is infringed upon.

104. Under certain conditions, the AIA considers a deployer to be a provider. It does so i.a. when the deployer modifies the intended purpose of certain AI systems.[195] However, as the example above illustrates, the inappropriate proxy might be chosen based on an unaltered defined intended purpose. Hence, this provision does not resolve the gap in the notion of accuracy in the AIA regarding the aspect of *proxy choice* for the deployer *in casu*.

4.3.1.D. Summary of Accuracy Requirements for High-Risk AI Systems

105. In summary, this chapter describes that the AIA requires HRAISs to be accurate in the following sense:

- Output maintaining a small distance to the proxy: the level of output accuracy must be appropriately high, i.e. the distance to the chosen proxy appropriately small (*traditional accuracy*);
- Appropriate high-quality input: systems are developed based on appropriate data regarding i.a. representativeness, being up-to-date and bias (*input accuracy*);
- Taking output-input relation into account: the output may not negatively influence accuracy in the future by impacting input (*feedback*);
- Proxy choice must be suitable for the intended purposes that you know, considering providers (*proxy choice*).

195 AIA art 25(1).

4.3.2. *Transparency-Related Accuracy Requirements*

106. The analysis now focuses on the next set of requirements: those on transparency for certain AI systems. The AIA requires that providers of certain AI systems that are intended to interact directly with natural persons, ensure that those systems:[196]

> 'are designed and developed in such a way that the natural persons concerned are informed that they are interacting with an AI system, unless this is obvious from the point of view of a natural person who is reasonably well-informed, observant and circumspect, taking into account the circumstances and the context of use.'

107. Depending on the output of the use-case, additional requirements might apply. Should the output not be a label indicating a range of mortality probability, rather a textual output, the provider would have to ensure it is outputted in machine-readable format and detectable as AI-generated or manipulated content.[197] Providers are required to do so concretely as follows: 'Providers shall ensure their technical solutions are effective, interoperable, robust and reliable as far as this is technically feasible, taking into account [i.a.] the generally acknowledged [SoTA], as may be reflected in relevant technical standards'.[198] Here again, the AIA refers to the SoTA. However, art 50 also refers to interpretation via codes of practice.[199]

108. As of this writing, no drafts of codes specifically addressing the aforementioned obligations have been published. There is however another AIA Code of Practice that is being developed: the GPAI Code of Practice. This book elaborates on the implications of that code, the GPAI CoP, in chapter 5.3.

4.3.3. *Requirements for GPAI: Models, Not Systems*

109. The AIA sets forth another set of requirements for GPAI models.[200] The regulation defines a GPAI model as an AI model that (i) 'displays significant generality', (ii) 'is capable of competently performing a wide range of distinct tasks' and (iii) 'can be integrated into a variety of downstream systems or applications'.[201] Here again the AIA provides a development exception like in art 2(8), excluding models 'used for research' or 'not yet placed on the market';

---

196 AIA art 50(1).
197 AIA art 50(2).
198 Ibid art 50(2).
199 AIA art 50(7).
200 AIA art 53 and 54.
201 AIA art 3(63).

unlike art 2(8) without carveout regarding 'testing in real world conditions'.[202] Once placed on the market, whether the use-case would constitute a GPAI model would depend on whether the system fulfils the three aforementioned conditions.

110. Considering the first two conditions, the AI Office states that '[t]raining compute is an imperfect proxy for generality and capabilities but currently the best metric for legal certainty' and '[its] preliminary approach is to presume that a model that can generate text and/or images is a [GPAI] model if its training compute is greater than 10^{22} FLOP.'[203] Provided that this interpretation would become final, the use-case need not constitute a GPAI model, as the provided recommendations are not necessarily text or images and the training compute did not exceed 10^{22} FLOP.[204]

111. The regulation does not define what AI models are, other than to say they 'are essential components of AI systems', but 'require the addition of further components, such as for example a user interface, to become AI systems'.[205] The AIA does define another concept, general-purpose AI systems (hereafter: GPAI systems): AI systems that are (a) based on a GPAI model and (b) have 'the capability to serve a variety of purposes, both for direct use as well as for integration in other AI systems'.[206] The use-case, depending on underlying technology, might entail a GPAI system. Be that as it may, it is of little consequence, because the AIA, via art 53 and 54, does not specify requirements regarding GPAI systems, only regarding GPAI models.[207,208] The interpretation of those articles is further specified via the GPAI CoP, which the analysis returns to in chapter 5.3.

---

202 AIA art 3(63).

203 European Commission, AI Office, *Targeted consultation in preparation of the Commission guidelines to clarify the scope of the obligations of providers of general-purpose AI models in the AI Act* (22 April 2025) 4.

204 Lengerich and others (n 12). In training the described AI system, the authors applied an algorithm to a data set including on the order of 10^5 subjects, in which about 10^2 features are recorded per subject. Their algorithm passes in the order of 10^2 times over the data set. Therefore, the training of their AI system consumed approximately $10^5 \times 10^2 \times 10^2$ FLOP = 10^9 FLOP.

205 AIA rec 97.

206 AIA art 3(66).

207 Except transparency requirements in art 50(2) and enforcement requirements in art 75(2).

208 The third GPAI CoP draft does add some nuance in Safety and Security section, Measure II.4.7, stipulating that providers of GPAISRs have some obligations on taking into account some foreseeable integrations of their GPAISR in GPAI systems. Nevertheless, these obligations directly address the provider of the GPAI model, not the provider of the GPAI system.

4.3.4. Additional Requirements for GPAI Models With Systemic Risk

112. Finally, the AIA also defines the category of GPAISR. Such a model is defined as a GPAI model that (a) 'has high impact capabilities evaluated on the basis of appropriate technical tools and methodologies, including indicators and benchmarks' or (b) 'based on a decision of the Commission, [...] has capabilities or an impact equivalent to those set out in point (a) having regard to the criteria set out in Annex XIII'.[209] Which is further specified as: '[a GPAI model] shall be presumed to have high impact capabilities pursuant to paragraph 1, point (a), when the cumulative amount of computation used for its training [exceeds 10^{25} FLOP]'.[210]

113. If a GPAI model is considered a GPAISR, art 52 up to and including 56 apply. The interpretation of those articles is further specified via the GPAI CoP, which the analysis returns to in chapter 5.3.

4.3.5. Mapping Accuracy Coverage in the AI Act

114. Bringing these requirements on aspects of accuracy together, this work first compares the requirements for each category of AI in Table 2. It excludes GPAI models and GPAISRs, because chapter 5.3 elaborates on them. Specifically, for HRAISs, Table 3 provides a comparison between the different requirements for providers and for deployers.

Table 2. Aspects of accuracy in the AI Act per AI category

Category	Traditional accuracy	Input accuracy	Feedback	Proxy choice	Subgoal robustness
AI practices in general					
AI systems with transparency obligations					
High-risk AI systems	*Art 15(1)* *Art 10(3)*	*Art 10(2)(c)* *Art 10(3)*	*Art 15(4)*	*Art 10(2)(a)* *Harmonised standards*	
(green: covered; orange: conditionally or partially covered; grey: not covered)					

[209] AIA art 51(1).
[210] AIA art 51(2).

Table 3. Aspects of accuracy for high-risk AI systems per actor

Actor	Traditional accuracy	Input accuracy	Feedback	Proxy choice	Subgoal robustness
Provider	*Art 15(1)* *Art 10(3)*	*Art 10(2)(c)* *Art 10(3)*	*Art 15(4)*	*Art 10(2)(a)* *Harmonised standards*	
Deployer		*Art 26(4)*			

(green: covered; orange: conditionally or partially covered; grey: not covered)

4.4. CASE STUDY: AN AI TRIAGE TOOL IN EU HOSPITALS

115. In the use-case the requirements relating to the aspect of *traditional accuracy* could potentially be fulfilled. What about the other aspects? In the use-case the used data set, consisting of historical data, has the appropriate statistical properties; the *proxy choice* impacts whether the confounder of historically given care pulls the output away from the actual goal. The impact of the confounder cannot be resolved by using other data. Hence, *input accuracy* requirements in art 10 are not necessarily infringed upon and as the input data is not the cause of the potentially undesired output, in terms of *input accuracy* the system could be regarded as accurate.

116. There is no learning in the operational phase of the system's lifecycle, so *feedback* is not present. The impact of the historically given care is hence not regulated by requirements regarding *feedback*. In terms of *subgoal robustness*, the AIA has no requirements, other than on certain GPAI models, which this work returns to in chapter 5.3. Be that as it may, as this system would lack the agentic capability to create subgoals, this aspect could potentially not be applicable.

117. That leaves *proxy choice*. Here the accuracy requirement has important nuances. The AIA's notion of accuracy might implicitly include *proxy choice*, but not under the requirements for deployers. Hence, there is a potential gap in the AIA's notion of accuracy, regarding *proxy choice*, in the requirements for deployers. In conclusion, the use-case might be accurate according to the AIA. Nevertheless, it might be inaccurate considering *proxy choice*.

5. BEYOND THE AI ACT: ACCURACY IN OTHER LEGAL FRAMEWORKS

118. Notions of accuracy are defined in other frameworks as well. This chapter analyses three other frameworks on their notion of accuracy: the GDPR, MDR and GPAI CoP. Here again, the analysis describes how those notions of accuracy cover the five key aspects of accuracy explored in chapter 3: (1) *traditional accuracy*, (2) *input accuracy*, (3) *feedback*, (4) *proxy choice* and (5) *subgoal robustness*.

5.1. GDPR: ENSURING ACCURATE INPUTS AND OUTPUTS

119. The GDPR also contains a notion of accuracy. Accuracy is already mentioned in art 5(1)(d):

> 'Personal data shall be: [...] accurate and, where necessary, kept up to date; every reasonable step must be taken to ensure that personal data that are inaccurate, having regard to the purposes for which they are processed, are erased or rectified without delay ("accuracy")'

120. This notion is also described in rec 71, which specifies that:

> 'the controller should use appropriate mathematical or statistical procedures [and] implement technical and organisational measures appropriate to ensure, in particular, that factors which result in inaccuracies in personal data are corrected and the risk of errors is minimised'

121. The mentioning of 'appropriate mathematical or statistical procedures' indicates that the aspects of *traditional accuracy* and *input accuracy* might be part of the GDPR's notion of accuracy. This does not however address *feedback*, *proxy choice* or *subgoal robustness*.

122. In *Google Spain SL and Google Inc. v Agencia Española de Protección de Datos (AEPD)*, the CJEU ruled that accuracy is a context-dependent notion.[211]

[211] Case C-131/12 *Google Spain SL and Google Inc. v Agencia Española de Protección de Datos (AEPD) and Mario Costeja González* [2014] ECLI:EU:C:2014:317 [72], [92] – [94]. The CJEU interpreted that data being 'kept up to date' includes it providing accurate information with regard to its function; which in the case shifted from 'accurate' news about a person, to 'inaccurate' illustration of the person's current situation.

The Court held that personal data can become inaccurate in relation to an ongoing function by the passage of time, thereby recognising temporal validity as part of accuracy in the GDPR.[212] Although the judgement was delivered under the Data Protection Directive (hereafter: DPD),[213] its reasoning remains authoritative under the GDPR, which preserves the same wording and structure in art 5(1)(d).[214] Both the CJEU and EDPB have continued to rely on DPD-era case law when interpreting GDPR provisions, confirming the doctrinal continuity between the two instruments.[215,216]

123. The EDPB has set up a ChatGPT Taskforce.[217] That taskforce published a report which states that '[i]n relation to the principle of data accuracy pursuant to Article 5(1)(d) GDPR, a difference should be made between input and output data'.[218] That dichotomy between input data and output data indicates that not only outputs are required to be accurate, but inputs as well. The report also refers to a judgement of the CJEU, which stipulates that the processing of personal data must comply with the 'principles relating to data quality' of i.a. GDPR art 5, further indicating the reference points to input data.[219,220]

124. The report also states that although information measures on 'the probabilistic output creation mechanisms [of ChatGPT,] are beneficial to avoid misinterpretation of the output, they are not sufficient to comply with the data accuracy principle'.[221] I.e., there is a requirement for the output to be accurate as well. Regarding the use-case, three different types of accuracy might be described: first, (i) accuracy of historical patient data for training and (ii) accuracy of current patient data for inference, measured against *de facto* patient variables, which are both part of *input accuracy*; and (iii) accuracy of the output measured with respect to a certain proxy, *traditional accuracy*.

---

212 Ibid [72], [92] – [94].

213 Directive 95/46/EC of the European Parliament and of the Council of 24 October 1995 on the protection of individuals with regard to the processing of personal data and on the free movement of such data (1995).

214 DPD art 6(1)(d); GDPR art 5(1)(d).

215 Case C-496/17 *Deutsche Post AG* [2019] ECLI:EU:C:2019:26 [57].

216 European Data Protection Board, *Report of the work undertaken by the ChatGPT Taskforce* (23 May 2024) [30].

217 European Data Protection Board, *Minutes 89th Plenary meeting* (16 January 2024) 2.

218 European Data Protection Board, Report of the work undertaken by the ChatGPT Taskforce (23 May 2024) [29].

219 Ibid [30].

220 *Deutsche Post AG* [57–58]. The case regards interpretation of requirements on data collection, i.e. input data.

221 European Data Protection Board, Report of the work undertaken by the ChatGPT Taskforce (23 May 2024) [31].

125. The GDPR does not directly address aspects of agentic AI systems and the aspect of *subgoal robustness* is not observed. In conclusion, Table 4 summarises the findings on the aspects of the notion of accuracy in the GDPR.

Table 4. Aspects of accuracy in the GDPR

Traditional accuracy	Input accuracy	Feedback	Proxy choice	Subgoal robustness
Art 5(1)(d) *Rec 71* *ChatGPT Taskforce*	*Art 5(1)(d)* *Rec 71* *ChatGPT Taskforce*			
(green: covered; grey: not covered)				

5.2. MDR: REQUIRING SAFETY AND PERFORMANCE FROM MOST

126. The MDR, as the AIA, divides medical devices into categories. As seen in chapter 4, these categories are: class I, class IIa, class IIb and class III. This work first analyses the category agnostic accuracy requirements, then analyses the class specific requirements.

127. The MDR lays down rules regarding the supply of medical devices on the Union market, including the first making available of the device in question, as well as the stage in which it is available for use 'for the first time for its intended purpose' to the final user.[222,223] The MDR defines different actors, i.a.: manufacturers, who manufacture and market the device in question;[224] authorised representatives, who hold a mandate to act on the manufacturer's behalf;[225] importers, who place a device from a third country on the market;[226] distributors, who make devices available on the market, who are not manufacturers or importers;[227] economic operators, who include manufacturers, authorised representatives, importers and distributors;[228] health institutions, organisations with the primary purpose of 'care or treatment of patients or the promotion of public health';[229] and users, who encompass healthcare professionals as well as lay persons who use the medical device.[230] The entity developing the

222 MDR art 1(1).
223 MDR art 2(27, 28 and 29).
224 MDR art 2(30).
225 MDR art 2(32).
226 MDR art 2(33).
227 MDR art 2(34).
228 MDR art 2(35).
229 MDR art 2(36).
230 MDR art 2(37).

AI triage tool in the use-case would be a manufacturer and hence an economic operator. The hospital would be a health institution.

128. Chapter II of the MDR stipulates obligations for economic operators, with respect to all medical devices. Those obligations include the requirement that all devices 'shall meet the general safety and performance requirements set out in Annex I which apply to it, taking into account its intended purpose'.[231] Those general safety and performance requirements (hereafter: GSPRs), include the requirement that the devices 'shall be safe and effective [...] provided that any risks [...] associated with their use [...] are compatible with a high level of protection of health and safety, taking into account the generally acknowledged [SoTA]'.[232] The GSPRs are not to be confused with the GPSR, the General Product Safety Regulation.[233] Here again like the AIA, the MDR links the requirements to the SoTA.

129. The MDR also refers to the SoTA and to harmonised standards in particular, in art 1, stating that the regulation shall apply to certain groups of products 'taking into account the [SoTA], and in particular existing harmonised standards for analogous devices with a medical purpose, based on similar technology'.[234] The MDR does not define the SoTA other than as above in art 1, but does contain a presumption of conformity based on harmonised standards, specifying that '[r]eferences in [the MDR] to harmonised standards shall be understood as meaning harmonised standards the references of which have been published in the [OJEU]'.[235]

130. The GSPRs include multiple requirements regarding accuracy. Devices are expected to be 'designed and manufactured in such a way as to remove or reduce as far as possible [...] risks [i.a.] from loss of accuracy of any measuring or control mechanism',[236] which is repeated explicitly for active implantable devices.[237] Furthermore, the requirements include that:[238]

> '[d]iagnostic devices and devices with a measuring function, shall be designed and manufactured in such a way as to provide sufficient accuracy, precision and stability

[231] MDR art 5(2).
[232] MDR Annex I (Chapter I) [1].
[233] Regulation (EU) 2023/988 of the European Parliament and of the Council of 10 May 2023 on general product safety, amending Regulation (EU) No 1025/2012 of the European Parliament and of the Council and Directive (EU) 2020/1828 of the European Parliament and the Council, and repealing Directive 2001/95/EC of the European Parliament and of the Council and Council Directive 87/357/EEC (2023).
[234] MDR art 1(2).
[235] MDR art 8(1).
[236] MDR Annex I (Chapter II) [14.2] (g).
[237] MDR Annex I (Chapter II) [19.1] (c).
[238] MDR Annex I (Chapter II) [15].

for their intended purpose, based on appropriate scientific and technical methods [and] limits of accuracy shall be indicated by the manufacturer.'

131. Additionally, 'instructions for use shall contain [...] specifications the user requires to use the device appropriately, e.g. if the device has a measuring function, the degree of accuracy claimed for it'.[239] Hence, *traditional accuracy* is covered for all classes, regarding economic operators.

132. Regarding manufacturers, the MDR sets forth additional requirements. It requires manufacturers to conduct a clinical evaluation.[240] That evaluation must abide by the requirements set out in art 61 and Annex XIV.[241] Those requirements include that manufacturers must provide sufficient clinical evidence of conformity with the GSPRs.[242] In conducting the clinical evaluation, manufacturers must 'appraise all relevant clinical data by evaluating their suitability for establishing the safety and performance of the device'.[243] In this case suitability might implicitly refer to two aspects of accuracy. Suitability can refer to input data quality: representativeness regarding intended patient cohorts, data being up to date, et cetera. Suitability can also refer to the appropriateness of the chosen target output: the proxy. Hence, here the MDR implicitly refers to both *input accuracy* and *proxy choice*.

133. Manufacturers must also implement a post-market surveillance system, which must abide by the requirements set forth in art 83.[244] That system could potentially catch inaccuracies that occur after putting the system on the market, during the deployment of the system.[245] Therefore, *traditional accuracy* remains monitored during that phase of the system's lifecycle. This in and of itself does not address *feedback*. As chapter 3 elaborates on, output might, e.g. in predictive policing, be 'confirmed' to be accurate due to a self-fulling prophecy.

134. Additionally, before placing the medical device on the market, manufacturers must perform a conformity assessment.[246] The manufacturer has different options depending on the device class. Details of the procedures themselves are described in Annexes II, III, IX, X and XI.

135. Conformity assessments can cover different aspects of a device, i.a. its design, its production, as well as involved organisations and individuals.[247]

239 MDR Annex I (Chapter III) [23.4] (h).
240 MDR art 10(3).
241 MDR art 10(3).
242 MDR art 61(1).
243 MDR art 61(1) and Annex XIV (Part A) [1](c).
244 MDR art 10(10).
245 MDR art 83(2).
246 MDR art 52(1).
247 Peter Cihon and others, 'AI Certification: Advancing Ethical Practice by Reducing Information Asymmetries' (2021) 2 IEEE Transactions on Technology and Society 12.

The procedure in Annex IX includes assessment of a quality management system (hereafter: QMS)[248] and of the technical documentation.[249] The QMS assessment requires the manufacturer to describe how the quality of the system is measured, including the techniques and data that arose in verifying the medical devices.[250] The technical documentation must include the performance of the device as specified in Annexes II and III.[251] Those specifications include i.a. results of validation tests intended to demonstrate conformity.[252] Here, the MDR refers again to *traditional accuracy.*

136. The procedure in Annex X is a form of type-examination.[253] It assesses the design of the medical device, including the technical documentation as described in Annexes II and III and a sample of the device production envisaged, also referred to as the 'type'.[254] The major difference with the procedure in Annex IX is the focus on the design in combination with a lack of an overall evaluation of the production. Content wise, regarding accuracy, they refer to the same technical documentation, referring similarly to *traditional accuracy.*

137. Analogously, the procedure in Annex XI differs from the procedure in Annex IX, in focussing on the production in combination with a lack of evaluation of the design.[255] Annex XI allows the evaluation to happen either by evaluation of the production itself,[256] or by evaluation of the manufactured products.[257] The production evaluation verifies i.a. that such production will yield products similar to the type described in the type-examination of Annex X.[258] The evaluation of the manufactured product similarly verifies that the production yields products similar to the type described in the type-examination of Annex X.[259] The difference lies in that not the production but the products themselves are evaluated.[260] In both forms of evaluation the output is compared to the proxy defined in the type-examination. Therefore, here again, the MDR refers to *traditional accuracy.*

138. Manufacturers of class III devices can use procedures specified in Annex IX or procedures specified in Annex X in combination with the

---

248 MDR Annex IX (Chapter I).
249 MDR Annex IX (Chapter II).
250 MDR Annex IX (Chapter I) [2.2].
251 MDR Annex IX (Chapter II) [4].
252 MDR Annex II [6].
253 MDR Annex X [1].
254 MDR Annex X [2].
255 MDR Annex XI [2].
256 MDR Annex XI (Part A).
257 MDR Annex XI (Part B).
258 MDR Annex XI (Part A) [6.2].
259 MDR Annex XI (Part B) [12].
260 MDR Annex XI (Part B) [14].

ones specified in Annex XI, i.e. procedures covering *traditional accuracy*.[261] Manufacturers of class IIb devices can use procedures specified in Chapters I and III of Annex IX, in combination with the procedure specified in Section 4 of Annex IX; or procedures specified in Annex X in combination with a procedure of Annex XI.[262] These combinations also cover *traditional accuracy*. For class IIa devices, manufacturers can use procedures specified in Chapters I and III of Annex IX, in combination with the procedure specified in Section 4 of Annex IX, or can draw up the technical documentation described in Annexes II and III in combination with performing a procedure described in Section 10 or 18 of Annex XI.[263] Again, *traditional accuracy* is covered. Manufacturers of class I devices can generally declare conformity themselves, in accordance with art 19 and with documentation specified in Annexes II and III, again including *traditional accuracy*.[264] In conclusion, all options for conformity assessment cover *traditional accuracy*, regardless of device class.

139. *Subgoal robustness* is not explicitly mentioned in the MDR. As the MDR does not directly address agentic systems like some HRAISs or GPAI systems, such may not be a most pertinent gap.

140. All the aforementioned MDR requirements apply to either economic operators or specifically manufacturers. None of these accuracy requirements necessarily apply to health institutions. The MDR foresees an exception for health institutions that are in-house manufacturers and meet the conditions set forth in art 5(5); only the GSPRs apply to those health institutions. See box 11 for the text of MDR art 5(5). The analysis above showed that the GSPRs include accuracy requirements. However, a health institution is not required to be an in-house manufacturer. Hence, provided that a health institution did not manufacture the device in-house they are (i) not manufacturers and (ii) not-inhouse manufacturers; therefore none of the aforementioned requirements apply.

141. In light of the absence of accuracy requirements applicable to health institutions that are not in-house manufacturers, similar to the AIA, issues might arise regarding *proxy choice*. As analysed in chapter 4, the AIA might not suitably cover *proxy choice* of HRAISs regarding deployers. That potential gap is echoed here in a lack of coverage of *proxy choice* regarding health institutions that are not in-house manufacturers.

261 MDR art 52(3).
262 MDR art 52(4).
263 MDR art 52(6).
264 MDR art 52(7).

142. In conclusion, Table 5 summarises these findings on the aspects of the notion of accuracy in the MDR, comparing the different actor types. Table 6 summarises the findings comparing the different medical device classes.

Box 11 – MDR art 5(5) – Placing on the market and putting into service

5. With the exception of the relevant general safety and performance requirements set out in Annex I, the requirements of this Regulation shall not apply to devices, manufactured and used only within health institutions established in the Union, provided that all of the following conditions are met:
   (a) the devices are not transferred to another legal entity,
   (b) manufacture and use of the devices occur under appropriate quality management systems,
   (c) the health institution justifies in its documentation that the target patient group's specific needs cannot be met, or cannot be met at the appropriate level of performance by an equivalent device available on the market,
   (d) the health institution provides information upon request on the use of such devices to its competent authority, which shall include a justification of their manufacturing, modification and use;
   (e) the health institution draws up a declaration which it shall make publicly available, including:
      (i) the name and address of the manufacturing health institution;
      (ii) the details necessary to identify the devices;
      (iii) a declaration that the devices meet the general safety and performance requirements set out in Annex I to this Regulation and, where applicable, information on which requirements are not fully met with a reasoned justification therefor,
   (f) the health institution draws up documentation that makes it possible to have an understanding of the manufacturing facility, the manufacturing process, the design and performance data of the devices, including the intended purpose, and that is sufficiently detailed to enable the competent authority to ascertain that the general safety and performance requirements set out in Annex I to this Regulation are met;
   (g) the health institution takes all necessary measures to ensure that all devices are manufactured in accordance with the documentation referred to in point (f), and
   (h) the health institution reviews experience gained from clinical use of the devices and takes all necessary corrective actions.

> Member States may require that such health institutions submit to the competent authority any further relevant information about such devices which have been manufactured and used on their territory. Member States shall retain the right to restrict the manufacture and the use of any specific type of such devices and shall be permitted access to inspect the activities of the health institutions.
>
> This paragraph shall not apply to devices that are manufactured on an industrial scale.

Table 5. Aspects of accuracy in the MDR regarding class agnostic requirements per actor type

Class	Traditional accuracy	Input accuracy	Feedback	Proxy choice	Subgoal robustness
Economic operators	*Art 5(2) GSPR*				
Manufacturers	*Art 2(35) + Art 83*	*Art 61(1) Annex XIV (Part A) [1](c)*		*Art 61(1) Annex XIV (Part A) [1](c)*	
In-house manufacturers health institutions abiding by art 5(5)	*Art 5(2) GSPR*				
Non-manufacturers health institutions					

(green: covered; orange: covered implicitly or via harmonised standards, blue: inherited; grey: not covered)

Table 6. Aspects of accuracy in the MDR regarding manufacturers per class

Class	Traditional accuracy	Input accuracy	Feedback	Proxy choice	Subgoal robustness
Class agnostic	*Art 5(2) GSPR Art 83*	*Art 61(1) Annex XIV (Part A)*		*Art 61(1) Annex XIV (Part A) [1](c)*	
Class I	*(As class agnostic) + Annex II*				
Class IIa	*(As class agnostic) + Annex IX or XI*				
Class IIb	*(As class agnostic) + Annex IX or Annexes X and XI*				
Class III	*(As class agnostic) + Annex IX or Annexes X and XI*				

(green: covered; orange: covered implicitly or via harmonised standards, blue: inherited; grey: not covered)

5.3. GPAI CODE OF PRACTICE: BALANCING ACCURACY AND OVERFITTING

143. The AIA provides multiple roads to further concretisation of its requirements. One is 'the generally acknowledged [SoTA], as may be reflected in relevant technical standards'.[265] The AIA also provides concretisation via a presumption of conformity that refers to certain harmonised standards.[266] When a standardisation request as described in AIA art 41 has been made and certain conditions on the sufficiency of the resulting harmonised standard have not been met, the Commission may adopt implementing acts establishing common specifications.[267] Another road to further concretisation comes via the codes of practice that providers of GPAI models may rely on.[268]

144. At the time of writing, there is a fourth draft of the GPAI CoP, expected to be the final version and to be adopted 2 August 2025.[269,270] The GPAI CoP is divided in '[c]ommitments by providers of [GPAI] models' on the one hand, and '[c]ommitments by providers of [GPAISRs]' on the other; explicitly so in the 3rd draft of the GPAI CoP, *de facto* still in the fourth draft: the 'Copyright Chapter' and the 'Transparency Chapter' apply to all providers of GPAI models, the 'Safety and Security Chapter' applies to providers of GPAISRs.[271]

145. Each part is structured on commitments, specified in measures.[272] While the second draft of the GPAI CoP did not mention accuracy explicitly, the third and fourth draft do and elaborate further on the implicit accuracy requirements that the second draft stipulated.[273]

146. The commitments regarding providers of all GPAI models contain two commitments: Copyright Chapter Commitment 1 on copyright and Transparency Chapter Commitment 1 on documentation.[274]

147. The commitment on documentation stipulates a measure on drawing up information specified in a 'Model Documentation Form', which includes

---

265 AIA art 50(2).
266 AIA art 40(1).
267 AIA art 41(1).
268 AIA art 53(4) for GPAI models and art 55(2) for GPAISRs.
269 4th GPAI CoP. European Commission, AI Office, *General-Purpose AI Code of Practice (Fourth Draft)* (final draft, 10 July 2025).
270 'The General-Purpose AI Code of Practice' (European Commission, 2025) <https://digital-strategy.ec.europa.eu/en/policies/contents-code-gpai> accessed 22 July 2025.
271 Ibid.
272 The second draft further specified these measures in KPI's; this is not the case anymore in the third and fourth drafts. 3rd GPAI CoP 4. 4th GPAI CoP.
273 European Commission, AI Office, *General-Purpose AI Code of Practice (Second Draft)* (working draft, 19 December 2024).
274 4th GPAI CoP Copyright Chapter 4, Transparency Chapter 5.

'[a] description of [measures] to address the prevalence of identifiable biases in the training data'.[275] The third draft additionally required the provider of GPAISRs to describe the used evaluation methods and metrics, this no longer forms part of the Model Documentation Form in the fourth draft.[276] It also includes a measure on providing the aforementioned information to the AI Office.[277] Therefore, *input accuracy* forms part of the notion of accuracy in the GPAI CoP regarding GPAI models and *traditional accuracy* formed part of the notion regarding GPAISRs in the fourth draft. It still forms part of the notion of accuracy in the fourth draft, but is moved to the Safety and Security Chapter.[278]

148. The commitment on copyright includes an aspect of accuracy that did not come up in the analyses of the other legal frameworks: overfitting.[279] It is implicitly mentioned in the AIA in the obligations regarding GPAI models.[280] The commitment in the GPAI CoP stipulates that providers commit to prevent that GPAI models will generate output sufficiently similar to input where it results in copyright infringement.[281] Here the distance between what is measured and to which variable it is compared should not be minimised, in other words: *qua* copyright-related overfitting high accuracy is undesirable.

149. The commitments regarding providers of GPAISRs describes a commitment on 'adopting a Safety and Security Framework'.[282] Measure 1.1 stipulates that '[t]he Framework will contain [...] a description and justification of the systemic risk acceptance criteria'. Measure 4.1 specifies that '[t]o do so, Signatories will [...] for each identified systemic risk [...] describe how they will [...] determine whether each identified systemic risk [...] and the overall systemic risk are acceptable', where the identified systemic risks are 'obtained through [...] compiling a list of risks [...] based on the [types of systemic risk in the appendix on systemic risk taxonomy].[283]

275 4th GPAI CoP Transparency Chapter, Measure 1.1, Model Documentation Form 9.
276 3rd GPAI CoP Transparency section, Measure I.1.1, Model Documentation Form 7. 4th GPAI CoP Transparency Chapter, Measure 1.1, Model Documentation Form 9.
277 4th GPAI CoP Transparency Chapter, Measure 1.2.
278 4th GPAI CoP Safety and Security Chapter, Measure 3.2.
279 The term 'overfitting' was used in the second GPAI CoP draft in measure 2.9 stipulating '[s]ignatories [...] commit to [...] prevent an overfitting of their [GPAI] model in order to mitigate the risk that a downstream AI system [...] generates copyright infringing output'. The third draft drops the term and rephrases the requirement in measure I.2.2 to 'ensure that Signatories will only reproduce and extract lawfully accessible works and other protected subject matter'. This work uses 'overfitting' for its succinct description of the matter.
280 AIA art 53(1)(c).
281 4th GPAI CoP Copyright Chapter, Measure 1.4.
282 4th CPAI CoP Safety and Security Chapter, Commitment 1.
283 4th CPAI CoP Safety and Security Chapter, Measure 2.1.

150. One of the systemic risk types in the taxonomy is the loss of control, specified as:[284]

> '[r]isks from humans losing the ability to reliably direct, modify, or shut down a model [which] may emerge from misalignment with human intent or values, self-reasoning, self-replication, self-improvement, deception, resistance to goal modification, power-seeking behaviour, or autonomously creating of improving AI models or AI systems.'

151. These propensities can be seen as a form of instrumental convergence, like Meinke et al. observed.[285,286] These commitments speak to *subgoal robustness*.[287] See box 12 for a comparison between capabilities and propensities.

> **Box 12 – Capabilities v Propensities**
>
> Assessments of AI models 'can be organised into two categories: (a) whether a model has certain dangerous capabilities, and (b) whether it has the propensity to harmfully apply its capabilities (alignment)'.[288] **Capabilities** speak to a model's abilities. **Propensities** speak to a model's inclination towards using its abilities in a certain way. Capabilities therefore are relevant for risks related to intentional misuse, as well as risks form unintended outcomes. Propensities on the other hand, regard how a model uses its capabilities regardless of whether a user intends to misuse the model.

152. The Safety and Security Chapter stipulates obligations for providers on assessing the systemic risk stemming from the GPAISRs throughout the models' lifecycle and conducting post-market monitoring.[289] The third draft, in commitments II.2, II.4 and II.8, included an obligation on reporting on data drift in updates of reports on the model's safety and security.[290] Data could drift because of a feedback loop or due to the reality it represents changing overtime. Hence, commitments II.2, II.4 and II.8, whilst not literally stating it nor being

---

284 4th CPAI CoP Safety and Security Chapter, Appendix 1.1, Appendix 1.4.

285 Bostrom (n 65) 7–8.

286 Meinke and others (n 3) 6–14.

287 This carves out obligations regarding *subgoal robustness* for providers of GPAI models without systemic risk; which were still present in the second draft of the GPAI CoP, in Commitment 3.

288 Google DeepMind, *Model evaluation for extreme risks* (23 May 2023) 2.

289 4th GPAI CoP Safety and Security Chapter, Measure 1.2.

290 3rd GPAI CoP Safety and Security section, Commitment II.2 on Systemic risk assessment and mitigation along the entire model lifecycle, Commitment II.8 on Safety and Security Model Reports, Measure II.4.14 on Post-market monitoring, Measure II.8.7 on Model Report updates.

limited to it, included prevention of impact of *feedback*. This is no longer present in the fourth draft.

153. Additionally, measure 3.2 stipulates that 'Signatories will conduct [...] model evaluations [...] ensuring [i.a.] internal [and] external validity'.[291] For demonstrating internal validity, a measure of evaluation accuracy in the test environment, the glossary prescribes i.a. 'controlling for confounding variables and mitigating spurious correlation' and 'preventing use of test data in training'.[292,293] The former refers to confounders, the latter to a form of output-input relationship. Therefore, *proxy choice* is covered by the notion of accuracy for GPAISRs.

154. This closes a carveout in the third GPAI CoP, where commitment II.8 only required non-SME GPAISR providers to document the internal and external validity of their model evaluations.[294,295] In other words, this closes the former gap exempting SME providers of GPAIRSs from considerations of *proxy choice*.

155. Whilst the accuracy aspect *feedback* is a form of output-input relationship as well, preventing the usage of test data in training does not necessarily imply output data is changing input data. Rather, the output might not be representative of the actual accuracy of the system, because the presence of test data in training data might undermine its ability to indicate the capacity of generalisation in a system. The following example illustrates this:

No test data usage in training

Training data	input: 1 + 2	output: 3
	input: 4 + 5	output: 9
Test data	**input: 5 + 3**	**output: 8**
Test	**input: 5 + 3**	**output: 8**

→ Test indicates model might generalise sums.

Test data usage in training

Training data	input: 1 + 2	output: 3
	input: 4 + 5	output: 9
	input: 5 + 3	**output: 8**
Test data	**input: 5 + 3**	**output: 8**
Test	**input: 5 + 3**	**output: 8**

→ Test is less indicative of model ability to generalise sums.

291 4th GPAI CoP Safety and Security Chapter, Appendix 3.1.

292 The fourth draft elaborates on the notion of internal validity in the glossary in the Safety and Security Chapter. The third draft no longer explained the concept of internal validity; the second draft did in Measure 10.3.

293 4th GPAI CoP Safety and Security Chapter, Glossary.

294 3rd GPAI CoP Safety and Security section, Commitment II.8.3(11). 3rd GPAI CoP Safety and Security section, Measure II.4.5.

295 This carved out obligations regarding *proxy choice* for SME GPAISR providers; which were still present in the second draft of the GPAI CoP, in Commitment 10. Similarly Measure II.4.10 described obligations regarding the prevention of test data usage in training, again only regarding non-SME providers of GPAISRs.

156. The prevention of test data usage in training is therefore not necessarily connected to *feedback*. It is a measure that is supportive of the indicative capability of a test. This work does not include it in the five aspects of accuracy mentioned in chapter 3. In the framework provided, this aspect could be added as the distance between training data and testing data. Similar to the commitment to prevent copyright-related overfitting, a small distance between the two data sets is undesirable.[296] Therefore, the framework with five aspects of accuracy overlooks aspects where distances between variables are desirable, rather than optimally minimised.

157. The third draft regarded all aspects of accuracy, but contained a gap regarding *proxy choice* of SME providers of GPAISRs. The fourth draft closes that gap, but opens a new one: *feedback* is no longer covered.

158. Additionally, this code regards the providers of GPAI models, not GPAI systems. Should a chatbot, i.a. ChatGPT, be considered to be a GPAI system, it would not therefore automatically fall within the scope of the GPAI CoP. There is an exception for providers of GPAI models that 'themselves provide and/or deploy AI systems that integrate their own model'; the GPAI CoP does require those providers to 'include monitoring the model as part of these AI systems'.[297] However, a chatbot provider integrating a third party GPAI model, would fall out of the scope of the GPAI CoP.

159. This chapter described how the aspect of *subgoal robustness* is covered for GPAISRs. However, *subgoal robustness* is potentially relevant whenever a model has the capability to create subgoals. Chapter 4 described how the determination of whether a GPAI model is regarded to have systemic risk is, at least in part, based on the size of the training compute. Barring any evidence of incapability of GPAI models with limited training compute to create subgoals, instrumental convergence could occur in models considered to be GPAI models without systemic risk. Therefore, the lack of regard to *subgoal robustness* in the GPAI CoP for such models forms a significant gap.

160. In conclusion, the GPAI CoP addresses multiple aspects of accuracy. As GPAISRs are always GPAI models,[298] the notion of accuracy applicable to them inherits the aspects of accuracy covered by the notion of accuracy for GPAI models in general. Table 7 summarises these findings.

---

296 The third draft of the GPAI CoP carved out obligations regarding test data usage in training for SME GPAISR providers, in Commitment II.8.3(11), which were still present in the second draft of the GPAI CoP, in Commitment 10.

297 4th GPAI CoP Safety and Security Chapter, Measure 3.5.

298 AIA art 51(1).

Table 7. Aspects of accuracy in the GPAI Code of Practice

Category	Traditional accuracy	Input accuracy	Feedback	Proxy choice	Subgoal robustness	Overfitting	Test data usage in training
GPAI		*Transparency Chap. M.1.1*				*Copyright Chap. M.1.4* *Regarding copyright too accurate outputs in terms of likeness to certain training data might be undesirable*	
GPAISR	*Safety and Security Chap. M.3.2*			*Safety and Security Chap. M.3.2 A.3*	*Safety and Security Chap. M.2.1 A.1*		*Safety and Security Chap. M.3.2 A.3* *Due to the ability of test data in training to undermine the indicative capability of testing its presence might be undesirable*

(Chapter, Commitment, Measure and Appendix are abbreviated respectively as "Chap.", "C.", "M." and "A."; green: covered; blue: inherited; grey: not covered)

6. REGULATORY BLIND SPOTS: UNCOVERED ASPECTS OF ACCURACY

161. This work described five key aspects of accuracy: (1) *traditional accuracy*, (2) *input accuracy*, (3) *feedback*, (4) *proxy choice* and (5) *subgoal robustness*. It then analysed which aspects are part of the notion of accuracy of the AIA. Additionally, it analysed which aspects are part of the notions of accuracy of the GDPR, MDR and GPAI CoP.

162. The analysis showed that the AIA does not have a singular notion of accuracy. Rather, it differs for the different categories of AI as defined by the AIA. It also differs for different actors that the AIA defines. Additionally, the notion of accuracy of the AIA is not in its entirety defined *within* the AIA; it is specified also in harmonised standards and the GPAI CoP.

163. The study established that the notion of accuracy of the AIA covers all five aspects of accuracy defined in chapter 3; however not equally for all categories of AI and all involved actors. For AI practices in general and AI with certain transparency requirements, little is defined in terms of accuracy. Other than AI literacy and aspects relating to whether all parties are aware that they are interacting with machine-generated content, requirements related to accuracy are limited.

164. The AIA covers more aspects of accuracy in its requirements for HRAISs and GPAI models, with and without systemic risk. For HRAISs, the analysis shows a difference between actors. Other than *subgoal robustness*, all aspects are covered in the requirements for providers. The aspect of *proxy choice* is not explicitly mentioned, but can implicitly be concluded from ISO13485, a harmonised standard, a source the AIA refers to for certain aspects of its interpretation. Whether *proxy choice* would be implied for all HRAISs is unclear, as there are multiple harmonised standards, and only ISO13485 was analysed in detail.

165. *Subgoal robustness* is inherently relevant only to systems capable of generating subgoals. Assuming that regulating *subgoal robustness* is deemed desirable specifically for GPAI systems, the analysis demonstrates that embedding such obligations within the requirements for GPAI models alone would not necessarily be sufficient. This insufficiency arises because GPAI model obligations do not directly and uniformly translate into requirements for GPAI systems.

166. Deployers of HRAISs must abide by less requirements relating to accuracy. Only the aspect of *input accuracy*, and only in part, is included in the notion of accuracy regarding requirements for those deployers. Because the other aspects, except for *subgoal robustness*, are covered in the requirements for providers, one might conclude that all aspects are covered when taking the entire economic ecosystem into account. However, as chapter 4 describes, some issues might arise regarding *proxy choice*.

167. The GDPR covers the more static aspects of accuracy: *traditional accuracy* and *input accuracy*. In and of itself that is not necessarily problematic, as the AIA can regulate certain aspects in parallel with the GDPR. For HRAISs that learn during the operational phase or are more agentic in nature, the AIA could potentially partially cover the remaining aspects.

168. The MDR addresses *traditional accuracy*, *input accuracy* and *proxy choice*. Like the AIA, it adopts a heterogeneous approach to accuracy, differentiating between actor types. The MDR echoes the AIA in its potential gap in the coverage of *proxy choice* for HRAISs regarding deployers. The MDR analogously considers *proxy choice* for MDSW primarily for manufacturers, leaving the deploying health institutions unaddressed.

169. For GPAI models, the notion of accuracy of the AIA is further defined in the GPAI CoP. The commitments described in that code cover all aspects described in chapter 3, except *feedback*. However, for GPAI models without systemic risk, also *traditional accuracy*, *proxy choice* and *subgoal robustness* are not covered. The fourth version of the code closes a former gap regarding *proxy choice* of SME providers of GPAISRs, but however opens a new gap regarding *feedback*.

170. Specifically for providers of GPAISRs *traditional accuracy* and *subgoal robustness* are directly covered, but that does not imply none of the other aspects are covered regarding those providers, as that category inherits the requirements for GPAI models in general.

171. Additionally, the GPAI CoP does not directly address implementations of GPAI models in AI systems. Therefore, a GPAI system is not necessarily regulated by either HRAIS requirements or GPAI model requirements.

172. In conclusion, multiple aspects of accuracy remain uncovered by the analysed EU legislation. The most pertinent gaps seem to be *proxy choice* for HRAISs, specifically regarding requirements for deployers; analogously *proxy choice* for MDSW, specifically considering the deploying health institutions; and *feedback* regarding providers of GPAI models. These challenges could potentially be addressed in part by (i) making the aspect of *proxy choice* operative in the accuracy requirements enshrined in art 15(1) and art 10(2)(a), and (ii) explicitly requiring deployers of HRAISs to appraise the *proxy choice* in relation to their *in concreto* implementation of the system. This could respectively be achieved by (i) including the aspect of *proxy choice* in the notion of accuracy in harmonised standards, and (ii) specifying in future AI Office guidance that appraisal of the proxy chosen by the deployer, in light of the *in concreto* intended purpose, forms part of the obligations for deployers set forth in art 26(1).

173. Additionally, GPAI systems largely fall out of scope of the GPAI CoP and AIA HRAIS requirements. This might be remedied by amending the AIA to incorporate obligations for providers of GPAI systems. Concretely, an article could be added requiring GPAI system providers to follow both HRAIS requirements and apply the GPAI CoP to their GPAI *systems*.

7. WHAT THIS BOOK MISSED

174. Naturally, this book missed everything that occurred after it was sent to the printer and the interpretation of the AIA evolves constantly. In August 2025 the GPAI CoP might be adopted, and January 2026 the Commission might have published its guidance on HRAISs.[299] Although this book assesses multiple frameworks, it is not exhaustive, i.a. the Data Act, Data Governance Act and General Product Safety Regulation are not covered.[300]

175. Nevertheless, this work elaborates on core concepts regarding AI accuracy and its regulation. Most of all, it provides a framework to assess accuracy, which can serve as both a new lens through which legislators can assess AI regulation, as well as a common language for legal and technical experts.

---

299 European Commission, AI Office, *Public consultation regarding guidelines for providers of high-risk AI systems* (6 June 2025).

300 Regulation of the European Parliament and of the Council on harmonised rules on fair access to and use of data (Data Act) (2022). Regulation (EU) 2022/868 of the European Parliament and of the Council of 30 May 2022 on European data governance and amending Regulation (EU) 2018/1724 (Data Governance Act) (2022). *Regulation (EU) 2023/988 of the European Parliament and of the Council of 10 May 2023 on general product safety, amending Regulation (EU) No 1025/2012 of the European Parliament and of the Council and Directive (EU) 2020/1828 of the European Parliament and the Council, and repealing Directive 2001/95/EC of the European Parliament and of the Council and Council Directive 87/357/EEC.*

8. LEGISLATOR, WHERE DO WE GO FROM HERE?

176. This book explored the aspects of accuracy in technical literature and how they are reflected in legal notions of accuracy regarding AI systems. Accuracy always describes two things: the distance between two variables and the choice of those variables. The aspects of accuracy which this work described focus on minimisation of distances. Copyright-related overfitting and usage of test data in training indicate that other aspects of accuracy can be relevant as well. Nevertheless, the analysis brought forth none such aspects that are generally seen as desirable. The work found five aspects of accuracy in technical literature: *traditional accuracy*, *input accuracy*, *feedback*, *proxy choice* and *subgoal robustness*.

177. The book analysed which of these aspects are covered by the notions of accuracy in the AI Act, GDPR, MDR and GPAI Code of Practice. The findings show that the AI Act does not itself describe its entire notion of accuracy. Regarding this, the AI Act refers to harmonised standards in two ways: art 8 and rec 121 define that obligations from the section regarding requirements for high-risk AI systems are to be applied through the lens of the state of the art, defined as harmonised standards; and art 40(1) refers to the standards via its presumption of conformity. Additionally, the GPAI Code of Practice acts as further specification for i.a. the notion of accuracy, regarding GPAI models.

178. The work showed that the AI Act differs in the aspects of accuracy covered in its notion of accuracy, both between the categories of AI it defines, as well as between the types of actors in question. Similarly, the GPAI Code of Practice differs in its coverage of aspects of accuracy i.a. between GPAI models without and GPAI models with systemic risk. The GDPR, analogous to the AI Act, includes a dichotomy between input and output accuracy and covers the two first aspects of accuracy: *traditional accuracy* and *input accuracy*.

179. The findings of this book illustrate potential gaps in those notions of accuracy, in particular: (i) the AI Act might not suitably cover *proxy choice* for high-risk AI systems, specifically regarding deployers; (ii) the MDR analogously contains a potential gap considering *proxy choice* for AI in medical devices when addressing the deploying health institutions; and (iii) the GPAI Code of Practice might not suitably cover *feedback* and *subgoal robustness* for providers of GPAI models. Additionally, chatbot providers remain partly unregulated, as GPAI systems can fall out of scope of both high-risk AI system requirements and the GPAI Code of Practice, leaving mainly transparency requirements. Finally, the book offers interpretative adjustments which could aid in making the aspect of *proxy choice* operative in the requirements enshrined in art 15(1), art 10(2)(a) and art 26(1) and could close the regulatory gap regarding GPAI systems.

BIBLIOGRAPHY

REGULATIONS, IMPLEMENTING DECISIONS AND NORMS

Council Directive 93/42/EEC of 14 June 1993 concerning medical devices (1993)

Directive 95/46/EC of the European Parliament and of the Council of 24 October 1995 on the protection of individuals with regard to the processing of personal data and on the free movement of such data (1995) OJ L 281/31

Regulation (EU) No 1025/2012 of the European Parliament and of the Council of 25 October 2012 on European standardisation, amending Council Directives 89/686/EEC and 93/15/EEC and Directives 94/9/EC, 94/25/EC, 95/16/EC, 97/23/EC, 98/34/EC, 2004/22/EC, 2007/23/EC, 2009/23/EC and 2009/105/EC of the European Parliament and of the Council and repealing Council Decision 87/95/EEC and Decision No 1673/2006/EC of the European Parliament and of the Council (2012)

Regulation (EU) 2016/679 of the European Parliament and of the Council of 27 April 2016 on the protection of natural persons with regard to the processing of personal data and on the free movement of such data, and repealing Directive 95/46/EC (General Data Protection Regulation) (2016) OJ L 119/1

Commission Implementing Decision (EU) 2021/1182 of 16 July 2021 on the harmonised standards for medical devices drafted in support of Regulation (EU) 2017/745 of the European Parliament and of the Council (European Commission 2021) OJ L256/100

Commission Implementing Decision (EU) 2022/6 of 4 January 2022 amending Implementing Decision (EU) 2021/1182 as regards harmonised standards for biological evaluation of medical devices, sterilisation of health care products, aseptic processing of health care products, quality management systems, symbols to be used with information to be supplied by the manufacturer, processing of health care products and home light therapy equipment (European Commission 2022) OJ L1/11

Commission Implementing Decision (EU) 2022/757 of 11 May 2022 amending Implementing Decision (EU) 2021/1182 as regards harmonised standards for quality management systems, sterilisation and application of risk management to medical devices (European Commission 2022) OJ L138/27

Proposal for a Regulation of the European Parliament and of the Council laying down harmonised rules on artificial intelligence (Artificial Intelligence Act) and amending certain Union legislative acts – General approach (2022)

Regulation (EU) 2022/868 of the European Parliament and of the Council of 30 May 2022 on European data governance and amending Regulation (EU) 2018/1724 (Data Governance Act) (2022) OJ L 152

Amendments adopted by the European Parliament on 14 June 2023 on the proposal for a regulation of the European Parliament and of the Council on laying down harmonised rules on artificial intelligence (Artificial Intelligence Act) and amending certain Union legislative acts (European Parliament, 2023)

Commission Implementing Decision (EU) 2023/1410 of 4 July 2023 amending Implementing Decision (EU) 2021/1182 as regards harmonised standards for sterilization of health care products and biological evaluation of medical devices (European Commission 2023) OJ L170/102

Regulation (EU) 2023/607 of the European Parliament and of the Council of 15 March 2023 amending Regulations (EU) 2017/745 and (EU) 2017/746 as regards the transitional provisions for certain medical devices and in vitro diagnostic medical devices (2023) OJ L 80/24

Regulation (EU) 2023/988 of the European Parliament and of the Council of 10 May 2023 on general product safety, amending Regulation (EU) No 1025/2012 of the European Parliament and of the Council and Directive (EU) 2020/1828 of the European Parliament and the Council, and repealing Directive 2001/95/EC of the European Parliament and of the Council and Council Directive 87/357/EEC (2023) OJ L 135

Commission Implementing Decision (EU) 2024/815 of 6 March 2024 amending Implementing Decision (EU) 2021/1182 as regards harmonised standards for medical gloves for single use, biological evaluation of medical devices, sterilization of health care products, packaging for terminally sterilized medical devices and processing of health care products (European Commission 2024) OJ L2024/815

Commission Implementing Decision (EU) 2024/2631 of 8 October 2024 amending Implementing Decision (EU) 2021/1182 as regards the harmonised standard for aseptic processing of health care products (European Commission 2024) OJ L2024/2631

Regulation (EU) 2024/1689 of the European Parliament and of the Council of 13 June 2024 laying down harmonised rules on artificial intelligence and amending Regulations (EC) No 300/2008, (EU) No 167/2013, (EU) No 168/2013, (EU) 2018/858, (EU) 2018/1139 and (EU) 2019/2144 and Directives 2014/90/EU, (EU) 2016/797 and (EU) 2020/1828 (Artificial Intelligence Act) (2024) OJ L 2024/1689

Commission Implementing Decision (EU) 2025/681 of 8 April 2025 amending Implementing Decision (EU) 2021/1182 as regards harmonised standards for medical gloves for single use, sterilization of medical devices and patient handling equipment used in ambulances (European Commission 2025) OJ L, 2025/681

Commission Implementing Regulation (EU) 2025/454 of 7 March 2025 laying down the rules for the application of Regulation (EU) 2024/1689 of the European Parliament and of the Council as regards the establishment of a scientific panel of independent experts in the field of artificial intelligence (European Commission 2025) OJ L2025/454

Regulation (EU) 2017/745 of the European Parliament and of the Council of 5 April 2017 on medical devices, amending Directive 2001/83/EC, Regulation (EC) No 178/2002 and Regulation (EC) No 1223/2009 and repealing Council Directives 90/385/EEC and 93/42/EEC (2017) OJ L130/18

Proposal for a Directive of the European Parliament and of the Council on adapting non-contractual civil liability rules to artificial intelligence (AI Liability Directive) (2022)

Regulation of the European Parliament and of the Council on harmonised rules on fair access to and use of data (Data Act) (2022)

Council of Europe Framework Convention on Artificial Intelligence, Human Rights, Democracy and the Rule of Law (2024)

European Commission, *Commission Guidelines on the Definition of an Artificial Intelligence System Established by Regulation (EU) 2024/1689 (AI Act)* (C(2025) 924 final 6 February 2025)

EN ISO 13485:2016/A11:2021, *Medical devices – Quality management systems – Requirements for regulatory purposes* (2021)

Council of the European Union, *Proposal for a Regulation of the European Parliament and of the Council laying down harmonised rules on artificial intelligence (Artificial Intelligence Act) and amending certain Union legislative acts – Fourth Presidency compromise text* (Council Document 13102/22 Interinstitutional File 2021/0106(COD), 19 October 2022)

European Commission, *Commission Implementing Decision (EU) of 22.5.2023 on a standardisation request to the European Committee for Standardisation and the European Committee for Electrotechnical Standardisation in support of Union policy on artificial intelligence* (C(2023)3215 22 May 2023)

CASE LAW

Lindqvist (Case C-101/01) [2003] ECLI:EU:C:2003:596

Brain Products GmbH v BioSemi VOF and Others (Case C-219/11) [2012] ECLI:EU:C:2012:742

Google Spain SL and Google Inc. v Agencia Española de Protección de Datos (AEPD) and Mario Costeja González (Case C-131/12) [2014] ECLI:EU:C:2014:317

James Elliott Construction Limited v Irish Asphalt Limited, (Case C-613/14) [2016] ECLI:EU:C:2016:821

Syndicat national de l'industrie des technologies médicales (SNITEM) and Philips France v Premier Ministre and Ministre des Affairs sociales et de la Santé (Case C-329/16) [2017] ECLI:EU:C:2017:947

Deutsche Post AG (Case C-496/17) [2019] ECLI:EU:C:2019:26

J.M. v Pankki S (Case C-579/21) [2022] ECLI:EU:C:2023:501

Meta Platforms Ireland Limited v Bundesverband der Verbraucherzentralen und Verbraucherverbände – Verbraucherzentrale Bundesverband e.V. (Case C-319/20) [2022] ECLI:EU:C:2022:322

Request for a preliminary ruling from the Landgericht Bochum (Germany) lodged on 18 June 2024 – Zentrale zur Bekämpfung unlauteren Wettbewerbs Frankfurt am Main eV v Diagramm Halbach GmbH & Co. KG (Case C/2024/5402) [2024]

Cassella-med GmbH & Co. KG, MCM Klosterfrau Vertriebsgesellschaft mbH v Verband Sozialer Wettbewerb eV (Case C-589/23) [2025] ECLI:EU:C:2025:173

JOURNAL AND CONFERENCE ARTICLES

Athindran Ramesh Kumar PJR, 'DiffLoop: Tuning PID Controllers by Differentiating Through the Feedback Loop' (CISS, Baltimore, MD, USA, 22 June 2021)

Biasin E, 'Why accuracy needs further exploration in data protection' (Proceedings of the 1st International Conference on AI for People: Towards Sustainable AI EAI, 13 December 2021)

Dylan Hadfield-Menell AD, Pieter Abbeel, Stuart Russell, 'Cooperative Inverse Reinforcement Learning' (NIPS, Barcelona, Spain, 5 December 2016)

Jason Wei XW, Dale Schuurmans, Maarten Bosma, Brian Ichter, Fei Xia, Ed H. Chi, Quoc V. Le, Denny Zhou, 'Chain-of-Thought Prompting Elicits Reasoning in Large Language Models' (NeurIPS, 2022)

Soares N and others, 'Corrigibility' (the Twenty-Ninth AAAI Conference on Artificial Intelligence, Austin, 25 January 2015)

Ahsan M, Luna SA and Siddique Z, 'Machine-Learning-Based Disease Diagnosis: A Comprehensive Review' (2022) 10 Healthcare 541

Amodei D and others, 'Concrete Problems in AI Safety' (2016) arXiv:160606565 [csAI]

Anoke SC, Normand S-L and Zigler CM, 'Approaches to treatment effect heterogeneity in the presence of confounding' (2019) 38 Statistics in Medicine 2799

Armstrong S, 'General purpose intelligence: arguing the Orthogonality thesis' (2013) 12 Analysis and Metaphysics 68

Bastos FB, 'Doctrinal Methodology in EU Administrative Law: Confronting the "Touch of Stateness"' (2021) 22 German Law Journal 593

Biasin E and Kamenjašević E, 'Regulatory Approaches Towards AI-Based Medical Device Cybersecurity: A Transatlantic Perspective' (2024) 15 European Journal of Risk Regulation 876

Biasin E, Yaşar B and Kamenjašević E, 'New Cybersecurity Requirements for Medical Devices in the EU: The Forthcoming European Health Data Space, Data Act, and Artificial Intelligence Act' (2023) 5 Law, Technology and Humans 43

Bostrom N, 'The Superintelligent Will: Motivation and Instrumental Rationality in Advanced Artificial Agents' (2012) 22 Minds and Machines 71

Cahan EM and others, 'Putting the data before the algorithm in big data addressing personalized healthcare' (2019) 78 npj Digital Medicine

Castle S, Schwarzenberg R and Pourvali M, 'Detecting Covariate Drift with Explanations' (2021) 13029 Natural Language Processing and Chinese Computing 317

Chang X, 'Gender Bias in Hiring: An Analysis of the Impact of Amazon's Recruiting Algorithm' (2023) 23 International Conference on Management Research and Economic Development 134

Cihon P and others, 'AI Certification: Advancing Ethical Practice by Reducing Information Asymmetries' (2021) 2 IEEE Transactions on Technology and Society 200

Dimitrova D, 'The Rise of the Personal Data Quality Principle. Is it Legal and Does it Have an Impact on the Right to Rectification?' (2021) 3 EJLT 1

Eichler H-G and others, '"Threshold-crossing": A Useful Way to Establish the Counterfactual in Clinical Trials?' (2016) 100 Clinical Pharmacology & Therapeutics 699

Ensign D and others, 'Runaway Feedback Loops in Predictive Policing' (2018) 81 Proceedings of Machine Learning Research 1

Fernández-Llorca D, Gómez E and Mazzini G, 'An interdisciplinary account of the terminological choices by EU policymakers ahead of the final agreement on the AI Act: AI system, general purpose AI system, foundation model, and generative AI' (2024) Artificial Intelligence and Law 1

Fraser AG and others, 'Artificial intelligence in medical device software and high-risk medical devices – a review of definitions, expert recommendations and regulatory initiatives' (2023) 20 Expert review of medical devices 476

Ghassemi M and others, 'A Review of Challenges and Opportunities in Machine Learning for Health' (2020) AMIA Jt Summits Transl Sci Proc 191

Harada S and Kashima H, 'InfoCEVAE: treatment effect estimation with hidden confounding variables matching' (2024) 113 Machine Learning 1799

Hung T-W and Yen C-P, 'Predictive policing and algorithmic fairness' (2023) 201 Synthese 201

Jiayi Lian LF, Hong Y and Deng X, 'Robustness with respect to class imbalance in artificial intelligence classification algorithms' (2021) 53 Journal of Quality Technology 505

Juson LV and Page BL, 'Calibrations of the Line Standards of Length of the National Bureau of Standards' (1934) 13 Journal of Research of the National Bureau of Standards 757

Kamenjasevic E and Biasin E, 'Does EU Medical Devices Directive Apply to Contact Proximity Tracing Apps?' (2020) EPLR 1

Karlafti E and others, 'Support Systems of Clinical Decisions in the Triage of the Emergency Department Using Artificial Intelligence: The Efficiency to Support Triage' (2013) 30 Acta medica Lituanica

Khanna VV and others, 'A machine learning and explainable artificial intelligence triage-prediction system for COVID-19' (2023) 7 Decision Analytics Journal 100246

Lengerich BJ and others, 'Death by Round Numbers: Glass-Box Machine Learning Uncovers Biases in Medical Practice' (2022) medRxiv

Lindstad S and Ludvigsen KR, 'When is the processing of data from medical implants lawful? The legal grounds for processing health-related personal data from ICT implantable medical devices for treatment purposes under EU data protection law' (2023) 31 Medical Law Review 317

Meszaros J and others, 'ChatGPT, Are You Lawfully Processing My Personal Data? GDPR Compliance and Legal Basis for Processing Personal Data by OpenAI' (2024) 233

Palmieri S, 'The Renewed EU Legal Framework for Medical AI' (2024) 15 European Journal of Law and Technology

Pan X and others, 'Frontier AI systems have surpassed the self-replicating red line' (2024) arXiv pre-print

Pavese F, 'How much does the SI, namely the proposed "New SI", conform to principles of the Metre Treaty?' (2014) 19 Accred Qual Assur 307

Rademakers FE and others, 'CORE-MD clinical risk score for regulatory evaluation of articial intelligence-based medical device software' (2025) 8 npj Digital Medicine

Sahiner B and others, 'Data drift in medical machine learning: implications and potential remedies' (2023) Br J Radiol

Valderas JM and others, 'Defining Comorbidity: Implications for Understanding Health and Health Services' (2009) 7 Annals of family medicine 357

van Bekkum M, 'Using sensitive data to de-bias AI systems: Article 10(5) of the EU AI act' (2025) 56 Computer Law & Security Review 106115
van Dijck G, 'Predicting Recidivism Risk Meets AI Act' (2022) 28 European Journal on Criminal Policy and Research 407
van Kolfschooten H and van Oirschot J, 'The EU Artificial Intelligence Act (2024): Implications for healthcare' (2024) 149 Health policy 105152
VanderWeele TJ and Shpitser I, 'On the definition of a confounder' (2013) 41 The Annals of Statistics 196
Wieland Brendel MB, 'Approximating CNNs with Bag-of-local-Features models works surprisingly well on ImageNet' (2019) ICLR
Machine Intelligence Research Institute, *Coherent Extrapolated Volition* (2004)

BOOKS

Barnard C and Peers S, *European Union Law* (third edn, Oxford University Press 2020)
Bostrom N, *Superintelligence: Paths, Dangers, Strategies* (Oxford University Press 2014)
Christian B, *The Alignment Problem: Machine Learning and Human Values* (W. W. Norton & Company 2020)
Hernandez JBR and Kim PY, *Epidemiology Morbidity And Mortality* (StatPearls Publishing 2025)
Kestemont L, *Handbook on Legal Methodology. From Objective to Method* (Intersentia 2018)
Russell S, *Human compatible. AI and the Problem of Control* (Allen Lane 2019)
Russell S and Norvig P, *Artificial Intelligence: A Modern Approach* (fourth edn, Pearson 2022)
Turner J, *Robot Rules: Regulating Artificial Intelligence* (Palgrave Macmillan 2019)

REPORTS

CEN-CENELEC Joint Technical Committee 21 'Artificial Intelligence', *Business Plan for JTC 21* (16 March 2022)
CEN/CENELEC, *CEN/CLC/TR 17894:2024, Artificial Intelligence – Artificial Intelligence Conformity Assessment* (2024)
CEN-CENELEC Joint Technical Committee 21 Working Group 3, *Information technology – Artificial intelligence (AI) – Bias in AI systems and AI aided decision making (ISO/IEC TR 24027:2021)* (17 December 2023)
European Data Protection Board, *Minutes 89th Plenary meeting* (16 January 2024)
European Data Protection Board, *Report of the work undertaken by the ChatGPT Taskforce* (23 May 2024)
Higl-Level Expert Group on Artificial Intelligence set up by the European Commission, *Ethics Guidelines for Trustworthy AI* (8 April 2019)
High-Level Expert Group on Artificial Intelligence, *The Assessment List For Trustworthy Artificial Intelligence (ALTAI) for self assessment* (17 July 2020)

European Commission, *White paper On Artificial Intelligence – A European approach to excellence and trust* (COM(2020) 65 final 19 February 2020)

OpenAI, *Deep Research System Card* (25 February 2025)

Medical Device Coordination Group, *MDCG 2019-11 Guidance on Qualification and Classification of Software in Regulation (EU) 2017/745 – MDR and Regulation (EU) 2017/746 – IVDR* (2019)

European Commission Joint Research Centre, *JRC 139430 Harmonised Standards for the European AI Act* (24 October 2024)

European Commission, AI Office, *General-Purpose AI Code of Practice (Second Draft)* (working draft, 19 December 2024)

European Commission, AI Office, *Approval of the content of the draft Communication from the Commission – Commission Guidelines on prohibited artificial intelligence practices established by Regulation (EU) 2024/1689 (AI Act)* (2 April 2025)

European Commission, AI Office, *General-Purpose AI Code of Practice (Fourth Draft)* (final draft, 10 July 2025)

European Commission, AI Office, *General-Purpose AI Code of Practice (Third Draft)* (working draft, 11 March 2025)

European Commission, AI Office, *Public consultation regarding guidelines for providers of high-risk AI systems* (6 June 2025)

European Commission, AI Office, *Targeted consultation in preparation of the Commission guidelines to clarify the scope of the obligations of providers of general-purpose AI models in the AI Act* (22 April 2025)

Anthropic, Redwood Research, New York Universiry, Mila-quebec AI Institute, *Alignment faking in large language models* (20 December 2024)

Google DeepMind, *Model evaluation for extreme risks* (23 May 2023)

European Commission Joint Research Centre, *JRC Technical Report: Analysis of the preliminary AI standardisation work plan in support of the AI Act* (2023)

Kenniscentrum Data & Maatschappij, *Ethische principes en (niet-)bestaande juridische regels voor AI. Een praktische gids* (October 2020)

Meinke A and others, 'Frontier Models are Capable of In-context Scheming' (*Apollo Research*, 16 January 2025)

ONLINE SOURCES

'Statement on AI Risk' (2023) <https://www.safe.ai/work/statement-on-ai-risk> accessed 27 February 2025

'AI Act' (*European Commission*, 2025) <https://digital-strategy.ec.europa.eu/en/policies/regulatory-framework-ai> accessed 16 June 2025

'The General-Purpose AI Code of Practice' (*European Commission*, 2025) <https://digital-strategy.ec.europa.eu/en/policies/contents-code-gpai> accessed 22 July 2025

Brown S, 'Why neural net pioneer Geoffrey Hinton is sounding the alarm on AI' (*MIT Sloan*, 2023) <https://mitsloan.mit.edu/ideas-made-to-matter/why-neural-net-pioneer-geoffrey-hinton-sounding-alarm-ai?utm_source=chatgpt.com> accessed 27 February 2025

CEN-CENELEC, 'Artificial Intelligence' <https://www.cencenelec.eu/areas-of-work/cen-cenelec-topics/artificial-intelligence/> accessed 28 January 2025

——, 'CEN/CLC/JTC 21/WG 3 Work programme' <https://standards.cencenelec.eu/dyn/www/f?p=205:22:0::::FSP_ORG_ID,FSP_LANG_ID:3125028,25&cs=1DA476872963BA59ED30E0D391D01B7D5> accessed 28 January 2025

Dastin J, 'Amazon scraps secret AI recruiting tool that showed bias against women' (*Reuters*, 2018) <https://www.reuters.com/article/world/insight-amazon-scraps-secret-ai-recruiting-tool-that-showed-bias-against-women-idUSKCN1MK0AG/> accessed 28 February 2025

Hinton G, 'Speech at the Nobel Prize banquet' (*The Nobel Prize Foundation*, 2024) <https://www.nobelprize.org/prizes/physics/2024/hinton/speech/> accessed 15 May 2025

Perrigo B, 'Meta's AI Chief Yann LeCun on AGI, Open-Source, and AI Risk' (*Time*, 2024) <https://time.com/6694432/yann-lecun-meta-ai-interview/> accessed 27 February 2025

ANNEX I – HIGH-RISK AI SYSTEM CONFORMITY ASSESSMENT REQUIREMENTS

AIA art 43 describes the options that providers of HRAISs have to demonstrate conformity with Chapter III, section 2 of the AIA. The article i.a. refers to the procedures in Annex VI and Annex VII. Annex VI describes a conformity assessment 'procedure based on internal control', hereafter: the Annex VI procedure.[301] Annex VII describes a procedure based on an 'assessment of the [QMS] and [...] technical documentation', performed by a notified body, hereafter: the Annex VII procedure.[302]

Art 43 divides HRAISs in four types: 'systems covered by the Union harmonisation legislation listed in Section A of Annex I', systems covered by the Union harmonisation legislation listed in Section B of Annex I, 'systems listed in point 1 of Annex III' and systems 'referred to in points 2 to 8 of Annex III'.[303]

Providers of HRAISs 'covered by the Union harmonisation legislation listed in Section A of Annex I', are required to (i) 'follow the relevant conformity assessment procedure as required under those legal acts', (ii) abide by and include in that procedure '[t]he requirements set out in Section 2' and (iii) perform '[p]oints 4.4., 4.5. and the fifth paragraph of point 4.6' of the Annex VII procedure.[304] The article sets forth no requirements regarding systems listed in Section B of Annex I.

To demonstrate compliance with the requirements set out in section 2, providers of HRAISs listed in point 1 of Annex III generally have multiple options. When 'the provider has applied the harmonised standards [(hereafter: HSs)] referred to in Article 40' in full, or has applied 'where applicable, common specifications referred to in Article 41', the provider can use either the Annex VI or Annex VII procedure.[305] Where (a) '[HSs] referred to in Article 40 do not exist, and common specifications referred to in Article 41 are not available [or] the provider has not applied them' or (b) 'the provider

---

301 AIA Annex VI.
302 AIA Annex VII.
303 AIA art 43(1, 2 and 3).
304 AIA, art 43(3).
305 AIA, art 43(1), first subpara.

has not applied [the HS in full]', he has to follow the Annex VII procedure.[306] Where the provider has applied a '[HS referred to in art 40 that] has been published with a restriction', he is required to apply the Annex VII procedure 'on the part of the standard that was restricted'.[307] Providers of HRAISs 'referred to in points 2 to 8 of Annex III' can use the Annex VI procedure.[308] Table 8 summarises these different options.

Table 8. Conformity assessment procedures for HRAISs

HRAIS type	Procedure
Section A of Annex I	(i) 'follow the relevant conformity assessment procedure as required under those legal acts' (ii) abide by and include in that procedure '[t]he requirements set out in Section 2' (iii) perform '[p]oints 4.4., 4.5. and the fifth paragraph of point 4.6' of the Annex VII procedure
Section B of Annex I	(no additional requirements)
Point 1 of Annex III	(a) Harmonised standards or common specifications AND (b) the Annex VI or Annex VII procedure (barring conditions)
Points 2 to 8 of Annex III	the Annex VI procedure

306 AIA, art 43(1), second subpara.
307 AIA, art 43(1), second subpara, point (d).
308 AIA, art 43(2).

ANNEX II – EVOLUTION OF HARMONISED STANDARDS UNDER THE MDR

As of today, the Commission has made seven implementing decisions on harmonised standards under the MDR:

- Commission Implementing Decision (EU) 2021/1182 of 16 July 2021.
- Commission Implementing Decision (EU) 2022/6 of 4 January 2022;
- Commission Implementing Decision (EU) 2022/757 of 11 May 2022;
- Commission Implementing Decision (EU) 2023/1410 of 4 July 2023;
- Commission Implementing Decision (EU) 2024/815 of 6 March 2024;
- Commission Implementing Decision (EU) 2024/2631 of 8 October 2024;
- Commission Implementing Decision (EU) 2025/681 of 8 April 2025.

The first implementing decision defined the first set of harmonised standards in art 1:[309]

> 'The references of harmonised standards for medical devices drafted in support of Regulation (EU) 2017/745 and listed in the Annex to this Decision are hereby published in the [OJEU].'

The decision sets the harmonised standards to:

1. EN ISO 10993-23:2021 Biological evaluation of medical devices – Part 23: Tests for irritation (ISO 10993-23:2021);
2. EN ISO 11135:2014 Sterilization of health care products – Ethylene oxide – Requirements for the development, validation and routine control of a sterilization process for medical devices (ISO 11135:2014)
   EN ISO 11135:2014/A1:2019;
3. EN ISO 11137-1:2015 Sterilization of health care products – Radiation – Part 1: Requirements for development, validation and routine control of a sterilization process for medical devices (ISO 11137-1:2006, including Amd 1:2013)
   EN ISO 11137-1:2015/A2:2019;

309 Commission Implementing Decision (EU) 2021/1182 of 16 July 2021 on the harmonised standards for medical devices drafted in support of Regulation (EU) 2017/745 of the European Parliament and of the Council (2021) art 1 and Annex.

4. EN ISO 11737-2:2020 Sterilization of health care products – Microbiological methods – Part 2: Tests of sterility performed in the definition, validation and maintenance of a sterilization process (ISO 11737-2:2019);
5. EN ISO 25424:2019 Sterilization of health care products – Low temperature steam and formaldehyde – Requirements for development, validation and routine control of a sterilization process for medical devices (ISO 25424:2018).

Later, the Commission adds the following harmonised standards:[310]

6. EN ISO 10993-9:2021 Biological evaluation of medical devices – Part 9: Framework for identification and quantification of potential degradation products (ISO 10993-9:2019);
7. EN ISO 10993-12:2021 Biological evaluation of medical devices – Part 12: Sample preparation and reference materials (ISO 10993-12:2021);
8. EN ISO 11737-1:2018 Sterilization of health care products – Microbiological methods – Part 1: Determination of a population of microorganisms on products (ISO 11737-1:2018)
   EN ISO 11737-1:2018/A1:2021;
9. EN ISO 13408-6:2021 Aseptic processing of health care products – Part 6: Isolator systems (ISO 13408-6:2021);
10. EN ISO 13485:2016 Medical devices – Quality management systems – Requirements for regulatory purposes (ISO 13485:2016)
    EN ISO 13485:2016/A11:2021;
11. EN ISO 14160:2021 Sterilization of health care products – Liquid chemical sterilizing agents for single-use medical devices utilizing animal tissues and their derivatives – Requirements for characterization, development, validation and routine control of a sterilization process for medical devices (ISO 14160:2020);
12. EN ISO 15223-1:2021 Medical devices – Symbols to be used with information to be supplied by the manufacturer – Part 1: General requirements (ISO 15223-1:2021);
13. EN ISO 17664-1:2021 Processing of health care products – Information to be provided by the medical device manufacturer for the processing of medical devices – Part 1: Critical and semi-critical medical devices (ISO 17664-1:2021);

---

310 Commission Implementing Decision (EU) 2022/6 of 4 January 2022 amending Implementing Decision (EU) 2021/1182 as regards harmonised standards for biological evaluation of medical devices, sterilisation of health care products, aseptic processing of health care products, quality management systems, symbols to be used with information to be supplied by the manufacturer, processing of health care products and home light therapy equipment (2022) art 1 and Annex.

14. EN IEC 60601-2-83:2020 Medical electrical equipment – Part 2-83: Particular requirements for the basic safety and essential performance of home light therapy equipment
EN IEC 60601-2-83:2020/A11:2021.

Later, amends No 10 to:[311]

EN ISO 13485:2016 Medical devices – Quality management systems – Requirements for regulatory purposes (ISO 13485:2016)
EN ISO 13485:2016/AC:2018
EN ISO 13485:2016/A11:2021

Also, then adds:[312]

15. EN 285:2015+A1:2021 Sterilization – Steam sterilizers – Large sterilizers;
16. EN ISO 14971:2019 Medical devices – Application of risk management to medical devices (ISO 14971:2019)
EN ISO 14971:2019/A11:2021.

Later, amends No 5 to:[313]

EN ISO 25424:2019 Sterilisation of health care products – Low temperature steam and formaldehyde – Requirements for development, validation and routine control of a sterilisation process for medical devices (ISO 25424:2018)
EN ISO 25424:2019/A1:2022

Then, also adds:[314]

17. EN ISO 10993-10:2023 Biological evaluation of medical devices – Part 10: Tests for skin sensitisation (ISO 10993-10:2021)

Later, adds the following:[315]

18. EN 455-3:2023 Medical gloves for single use – Part 3: Requirements and testing for biological evaluation;

---

311 Commission Implementing Decision (EU) 2022/757 of 11 May 2022 amending Implementing Decision (EU) 2021/1182 as regards harmonised standards for quality management systems, sterilisation and application of risk management to medical devices (2022) art 1 and Annex.

312 Ibid art 1 and Annex.

313 Commission Implementing Decision (EU) 2023/1410 of 4 July 2023 amending Implementing Decision (EU) 2021/1182 as regards harmonised standards for sterilization of health care products and biological evaluation of medical devices (2023) art 1 and Annex.

314 Ibid art 1 and Annex.

315 Commission Implementing Decision (EU) 2024/815 of 6 March 2024 amending Implementing Decision (EU) 2021/1182 as regards harmonised standards for medical gloves for single use, biological evaluation of medical devices, sterilization of health care products, packaging for terminally sterilized medical devices and processing of health care products (2024) art 1 and Annex.

19. EN ISO 10993-15:2023 Biological evaluation of medical devices – Part 15: Identification and quantification of degradation products from metals and alloys (ISO 10993-15:2019);
20. EN ISO 10993-17:2023 Biological evaluation of medical devices – Part 17: Toxicological risk assessment of medical device constituents (ISO 10993-17:2023);
21. EN ISO 10993-18:2020 Biological evaluation of medical devices – Part 18: Chemical characterization of medical device materials within a risk management process (ISO 10993-18:2020)
    EN ISO 10993-18:2020/A1:2023;
22. EN ISO 11137-2:2015 Sterilization of health care products – Radiation – Part 2: Establishing the sterilization dose (ISO 11137-2:2013)
    EN ISO 11137-2:2015/A1:2023;
23. EN ISO 11607-1:2020 Packaging for terminally sterilized medical devices – Part 1: Requirements for materials, sterile barrier systems and packaging systems (ISO 11607-1:2019)
    EN ISO 11607-1:2020/A1:2023;
24. EN ISO 11607-2:2020 Packaging for terminally sterilized medical devices – Part 2: Validation requirements for forming, sealing and assembly processes (ISO 11607-2:2019)
    EN ISO 11607-2:2020/A1:2023;
25. EN ISO 17664-2:2023 Processing of health care products – Information to be provided by the medical device manufacturer for the processing of medical devices – Part 2: Non-critical medical devices (ISO 17664-2:2021).

Thereafter, adds:[316]

26. EN ISO 13408-1:2024 Aseptic processing of health care products – Part 1: General requirements (ISO 13408-1:2023)

Finally, the last amendment as of this writing adds:[317]

27. EN 445-1:2020+A2:2024
    Medical gloves for single use – Part 1: Requirements and testing for freedom of holes;
28. EN 455-2:2024
    Medical gloves for single use – Part 2: Requirements and testing for physical properties;

316 Commission Implementing Decision (EU) 2024/2631 of 8 October 2024 amending Implementing Decision (EU) 2021/1182 as regards the harmonised standard for aseptic processing of health care products (2024) art 1 and Annex.

317 Commission Implementing Decision (EU) 2025/681 of 8 April 2025 amending Implementing Decision (EU) 2021/1182 as regards harmonised standards for medical gloves for single use, sterilization of medical devices and patient handling equipment used in ambulances (2025).

29. EN 556-1:2024
    Sterilization of medical devices – Requirements for medical devices to be designated "STERILE" – Part 1: Requirements for terminally sterilized medical devices;
30. EN 556-2:2024
    Sterilization of medical devices – Requirements for medical devices to be designated "STERILE" – Part 2: Requirements for aseptically processed medical devices;
31. EN 1865-2:2024
    Patient handling equipment used in ambulances – Part 2: Power assisted stretcher;
32. EN 1865-6:2024
    Patient handling equipment used in ambulances – Part 6: Powered chairs'.

Consolidated, the actual list, as of this writing, is the following:

1. EN ISO 10993-23:2021 Biological evaluation of medical devices – Part 23: Tests for irritation (ISO 10993-23:2021);
2. EN ISO 11135:2014 Sterilization of health care products – Ethylene oxide – Requirements for the development, validation and routine control of a sterilization process for medical devices (ISO 11135:2014)
   EN ISO 11135:2014/A1:2019;
3. EN ISO 11137-1:2015 Sterilization of health care products – Radiation – Part 1: Requirements for development, validation and routine control of a sterilization process for medical devices (ISO 11137-1:2006, including Amd 1:2013)
   EN ISO 11137-1:2015/A2:2019;
4. EN ISO 11737-2:2020 Sterilization of health care products – Microbiological methods – Part 2: Tests of sterility performed in the definition, validation and maintenance of a sterilization process (ISO 11737-2:2019);
5. EN ISO 25424:2019 Sterilisation of health care products – Low temperature steam and formaldehyde – Requirements for development, validation and routine control of a sterilisation process for medical devices (ISO 25424:2018)
   EN ISO 25424:2019/A1:2022;
6. EN ISO 10993-9:2021 Biological evaluation of medical devices – Part 9: Framework for identification and quantification of potential degradation products (ISO 10993-9:2019);
7. EN ISO 10993-12:2021 Biological evaluation of medical devices – Part 12: Sample preparation and reference materials (ISO 10993-12:2021);
8. EN ISO 11737-1:2018 Sterilization of health care products – Microbiological methods – Part 1: Determination of a population of microorganisms on products (ISO 11737-1:2018)
   EN ISO 11737-1:2018/A1:2021;

9. EN ISO 13408-6:2021 Aseptic processing of health care products – Part 6: Isolator systems (ISO 13408-6:2021);
10. EN ISO 13485:2016 Medical devices – Quality management systems – Requirements for regulatory purposes (ISO 13485:2016)
    EN ISO 13485:2016/AC:2018
    EN ISO 13485:2016/A11:2021;
11. EN ISO 14160:2021 Sterilization of health care products – Liquid chemical sterilizing agents for single-use medical devices utilizing animal tissues and their derivatives – Requirements for characterization, development, validation and routine control of a sterilization process for medical devices (ISO 14160:2020);
12. EN ISO 15223-1:2021 Medical devices – Symbols to be used with information to be supplied by the manufacturer – Part 1: General requirements (ISO 15223-1:2021);
13. EN ISO 17664-1:2021 Processing of health care products – Information to be provided by the medical device manufacturer for the processing of medical devices – Part 1: Critical and semi-critical medical devices (ISO 17664-1:2021);
14. EN IEC 60601-2-83:2020 Medical electrical equipment – Part 2-83: Particular requirements for the basic safety and essential performance of home light therapy equipment
    EN IEC 60601-2-83:2020/A11:2021;
15. EN 285:2015+A1:2021 Sterilization – Steam sterilizers – Large sterilizers;
16. EN ISO 14971:2019 Medical devices – Application of risk management to medical devices (ISO 14971:2019)
    EN ISO 14971:2019/A11:2021;
17. EN ISO 10993-10:2023 Biological evaluation of medical devices – Part 10: Tests for skin sensitisation (ISO 10993-10:2021);
18. EN 455-3:2023 Medical gloves for single use – Part 3: Requirements and testing for biological evaluation;
19. EN ISO 10993-15:2023 Biological evaluation of medical devices – Part 15: Identification and quantification of degradation products from metals and alloys (ISO 10993-15:2019);
20. EN ISO 10993-17:2023 Biological evaluation of medical devices – Part 17: Toxicological risk assessment of medical device constituents (ISO 10993-17:2023);
21. EN ISO 10993-18:2020 Biological evaluation of medical devices – Part 18: Chemical characterization of medical device materials within a risk management process (ISO 10993-18:2020)
    EN ISO 10993-18:2020/A1:2023;
22. EN ISO 11137-2:2015 Sterilization of health care products – Radiation – Part 2: Establishing the sterilization dose (ISO 11137-2:2013)
    EN ISO 11137-2:2015/A1:2023;

23. EN ISO 11607-1:2020 Packaging for terminally sterilized medical devices – Part 1: Requirements for materials, sterile barrier systems and packaging systems (ISO 11607-1:2019)
EN ISO 11607-1:2020/A1:2023;
24. EN ISO 11607-2:2020 Packaging for terminally sterilized medical devices – Part 2: Validation requirements for forming, sealing and assembly processes (ISO 11607-2:2019)
EN ISO 11607-2:2020/A1:2023;
25. EN ISO 17664-2:2023 Processing of health care products – Information to be provided by the medical device manufacturer for the processing of medical devices – Part 2: Non-critical medical devices (ISO 17664-2:2021);
26. EN ISO 13408-1:2024 Aseptic processing of health care products – Part 1: General requirements (ISO 13408-1:2023);
27. EN 445-1:2020+A2:2024
Medical gloves for single use – Part 1: Requirements and testing for freedom of holes;
28. EN 455-2:2024
Medical gloves for single use – Part 2: Requirements and testing for physical properties;
29. EN 556-1:2024
Sterilization of medical devices – Requirements for medical devices to be designated "STERILE" – Part 1: Requirements for terminally sterilized medical devices;
30. EN 556-2:2024
Sterilization of medical devices – Requirements for medical devices to be designated "STERILE" – Part 2: Requirements for aseptically processed medical devices;
31. EN 1865-2:2024
Patient handling equipment used in ambulances – Part 2: Power assisted stretcher;
32. EN 1865-6:2024
Patient handling equipment used in ambulances – Part 6: Powered chairs'.

INDEX